NORWICH'S MILITARY LEGACY

MICHAEL CHANDLER

Pen & Sword
MILITARY

To Ross

First published in Great Britain in 2017 by
PEN AND SWORD MILITARY
an imprint of
Pen and Sword Books Ltd
47 Church Street
Barnsley
South Yorkshire S70 2AS

Copyright © Michael Chandler, 2017

ISBN 978 1 52670 774 1

The right of Michael Chandler to be identified as the author of this work
has been asserted in accordance with the Copyright, Designs and Patents Act 1988.

Typeset by Aura Technology and Software Services, India

Printed and bound by CPI Group (UK) Ltd, Croydon, CR0 4YY

Pen & Sword Books Ltd incorporates the imprints of Pen & Sword
Archaeology, Atlas, Aviation, Battleground, Discovery, Family History, History, Maritime,
Military, Naval, Politics, Railways, Select, Social History, Transport, True Crime, Claymore Press,
Frontline Books, Leo Cooper, Praetorian Press, Remember When, Seaforth Publishing and Wharncliffe.

For a complete list of Pen and Sword titles please contact
Pen and Sword Books Limited
47 Church Street, Barnsley, South Yorkshire, S70 2AS, England
email: enquiries@pen-and-sword.co.uk
website: www.pen-and-sword.co.uk

CONTENTS

Introduction   4

1. A Potted Blog   11

2. Call to Arms: Pre-1899   25

3. Call to Arms: Post 1899   46

4. They Served   89

5. Regiments and Squadrons   103

6. Barracks and Buildings   109

7. Lest We Forget   114

    Sources & Acknowledgements   127

    About The Author   128

INTRODUCTION

Was the whole county about to be invaded in 1904? It became apparent after fishermen from Mundesley spotted ten first-class and four second-class battleships, and three armoured cruisers. It was claimed that over 10,000 German army personnel were on board. A full story of events was published as a Christmas story in the *Norwich Mercury*. It seems that, even in days gone by, reporters had the imagination to mix facts with fiction.

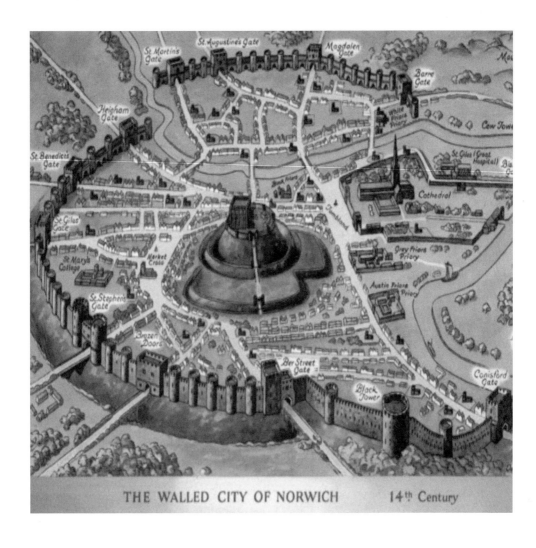

THE WALLED CITY OF NORWICH   14th Century

Many a time the castle of Norwich has looked down on the town to see riots in the streets, shops and houses burning, people killed and the byways full of rebels. During the Iron Age, East Anglia was in the hands of Celts. Called the Iceni, the most famous was Queen Boudicca, but it has always proved difficult pinpointing the exact location of the area she ruled. When her husband, King Prasutagus died the Romans took control with their large forces of occupation and used their power to raise taxes. Boudicca led her armies in rebellion, initially successfully, but she was captured and tortured and her daughters were raped. She escaped, but ultimately took her own life with poison.

The Romans had to keep the Iceni under control, so they built the town Venta Icenorum (Market of the Iceni) just a few miles south of Norwich on the River Tas. The Romans maintained military control until around 410 AD when the Anglo-Saxons began infiltrating the region vacated by the departing Romans, eventually gaining a hold in the area that would become known as Norwich. The occupation principally took place over four distinct districts: Norwich, Coslany, Westwick and Conesford.

Then came the longboats as Viking ships made their way up the River Yare raiding and pillaging. In 866, the Norsemen invaded East Anglia, and the same year, a large army fixed their winter camp in East Anglia where the inhabitants were subjugated. However, as wars were quickly won and lost, East Anglia ultimately fell into the hands of the Saxon king Edward the Elder in 917, but many Vikings stayed on in the area, settled and assimilated. Their influence is still with us today. However, fresh waves of Vikings continued to raid and plunder. In 1004, Sweyne came with his fleet to Norwich, burning and looting. The area was rebuilt, and some kind of normal life continued to exist until the Normans arrived in 1066. They came to an area that had 25 churches and over 5,000 residents. Where Ber Street ended, the Normans cleared the area and built a timber fortress that would become a royal castle.

Within a few years, a military plot against the king took place, staged by the Earl of Norwich, Ralph Guader, but the army stayed loyal to the king. Ralph escaped to Denmark to seek help, leaving his wife Emma to defend the castle, but within three months, she surrendered and the king again took power in Norwich.

Strife in various forms continued, but Norwich became stable enough to receive a Royal charter in 1158 from King Henry II, and another in 1194 from Richard I, the Lionheart.

During the Middle Ages, there were many conflicts. A group of barons decided to rebel against John I in 1215, inviting the French prince Louis to seize the throne. Louis at first captured Norwich Castle in 1217 before pillaging the entire area. This was repeated by the barons in 1266.

By 1253, Norwich's defences were enlarged with the addition of a new bank and a ditch. This led to conflict between Norwich and the priory, staffed with some very aggressive monks. In 1297, work started on building the defences that became the city walls, and which took nearly thirty-seven years to complete.

Common enclosures that had come into being by 1549 led to the Kett's Rebellion, which was instigated by brothers Robert and William Kett. The rebellion lasted three weeks with the rebels taking over the city and ending with the execution of the brothers in December the same year.

During the Civil War, Norwich came out in support of the Commonwealth and provided Cromwell's famous Maiden Troops.

By the end of the eighteenth century all the city gates had been demolished.

At the outset of the First World War, Norwich companies Mann Egerton, and Boulton & Paul were producing aircraft. In 1915, a seaplane, built by Mann Egerton, attacked and destroyed a Turkish freighter that was carrying supplies to Turkish troops at Gallipoli. Boulton & Paul produced over 2,500 aircraft.

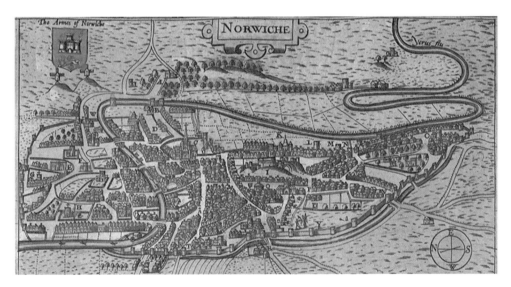

The medieval city of Norwiche.

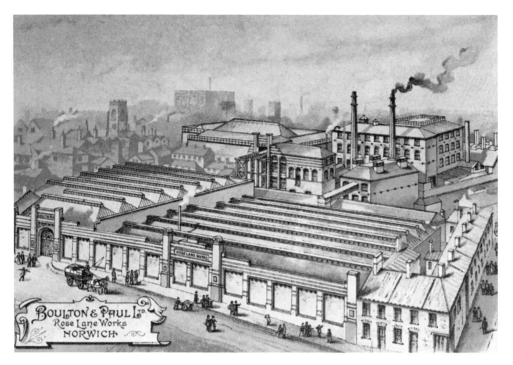

The Boulton & Paul Rose Lane Works in the 19th century.

Norwich companies that contributed to the war effort during the First World War included Howlett & White Ltd who provided 453,000 pairs of boots and shoes to the British army, 32,000 pairs to Allied armies and 21,000 pairs of aviation boots to the RAF. They also made boots for Cossacks.

Chamberlin & Sons clothing company made almost one million garments during the war, building and equipping a new factory in Norwich to meet demand. Its waterproofs were regarded as the best in the world. The War Office requisitioned its entire stock to provide oilskins for the troops.

P. Haldinstein & Sons took a leading role in making boots for soldiers. More than half a million pairs were produced. The workforce also raised large sums of money for entertainment for the wounded being treated in Norwich. The company went on to become Bally Shoes.

Shoe manufacturer Edwards & Holmes Ltd, although not directly engaged in war production, made many thousands of uppers for Cossack boots in 1915.

Mr Witton, of the highly regarded shoe company, S. L. Witton Ltd, and a member of the War Volunteer Fire Brigade, thought Norwich needed a new ambulance so he bought one and gave it to the Watch Committee on condition that they provided a new motorized fire engine. They did.

Wm. Hurrell's Phoenix Works took on government contracts to manufacture shoes for military rest camps and hospitals. The first order was for 40,000 pairs.

Wm. George & Sons, tanners, curriers and leather merchants, in St Benedict's, Pottergate, made a wide range of leather goods for the troops.

Barnard, Bishop & Barnards, Norfolk Iron Works weaved wire netting. During the first three years of the war, it made and supplied 12,310,435 yards – almost 7,000 miles – to be used in the trenches as bomb shields and for transport tracking over desert sands. It also produced hand-woven wire lattice for the Balkans theatre, large heating stoves for the US army, wire screens for high-explosive factories, hundreds of tons of castings for the Admiralty and other departments, cooking ranges, and heating stoves for camps and training centres.

Jarrold & Sons Ltd produced many notable books, including *The Blinded Soldier*, prepared and published in aid of St Dunstan's Home for Blinded Soldiers, *Told in the Huts*, *Shell Shocks*, and numerous guides for Australian and New Zealand troops sojourning in the 'old country' during the conflict.

Caley's produced 'Marching Chocolate' chocolate bars for troops at the front.

Norwich grocers Copeman's ran canteens, provided rations for the War Office and supplied rations for up to 30,000 troops in Norfolk.

BRCS Norwich Transport Company collected the wounded from Thorpe Station, Norwich, and ran them to the Norfolk & Norwich Hospital, or other sites.

Clothing company F. W. Harmer produced military uniforms.

As part of Norwich's defences against night-time attacks, was the requirement to put out the lights. This came about after the airship raids of January 1915. It was ordered:

a. That all outside lights, other than those maintained by the Corporation and Railway Companies, shall forthwith be kept extinguished.
b. That all the lights inside any building, whatsoever, excepting churches, shall be extinguished are [sic] covered by blinds or are constructed of such material as will effectually prevent light diffusing through them.
c. That in the case of factories with glass roofs, care must be taken to screen all lamps, whether gas, electric or oil, in such a way that the light shall not appear through the roof.

Men of the 1st Battalion, Norfolk Regiment on parade and being inspected by Sir John Anderson, the Governor General of Bengal, in Dacca, India, 1933. (Photo courtesy of Brian Harrington Spier)

Even though over 20,000 copies of the order were sent out in the city, it is hard to believe that a total of 4,042 Norwich citizens broke the order and were fined up to ten shillings for doing so.

At the time of researching this book, final preparations were under way as the city was getting ready to mark Battle of Britain Day, with a parade set for Monday, 12 September 2016 at 11.30 a.m. A parade by RAF Marham would be accompanied by the band of the Royal Air Force College in front of City Hall, watched by the Lord Mayor of Norwich, Councillor Marion Maxwell. A Spitfire would fly past at midday and a service was to be held the following Sunday at Norwich Cathedral. Lace panels, made by a firm in Nottingham and used by the Allies, would be on permanent loan to the cathedral. The panels took nearly two years to be designed and produced. Weighing nearly a ton, up to 40,000 cards were used. Thirty-eight panels were ultimately manufactured. Its next home was the officers' mess at RAF Coltishall. Funding for the move came from local benefactors and the manufacturers Babcock DynCorp, who further helped by giving technical assistance. The Battle of Britain panel depicts scenes from the battle and the many aircraft flown, including Spitfires, Hurricanes, Defiants, Messerschmitts, Stukas and Dorniers. Also included are the firefighters, anti-aircraft guns and searchlights.

The manufacturer's name, Dobson & Browne, is also shown, along with the designer's name, Harry Cross, and the draftsmen J. W. Herod and W. J. Jackson. One panel shows a cottage alongside a mansion, to highlight that both rich and poor suffered equally during the conflict. Also shown are Tudor roses, thistles, daffodils, shamrocks, acorns and oak leaves. Landmarks also appear, such as Buckingham Palace, St Paul's Cathedral, the Old Bailey, City Temple in Holborn, Bow Church, RAF Church St Clement Danes, Guildhall and the Houses of Parliament. Also depicted are the badges of the Allied air forces and the floral emblems of Great Britain and the Commonwealth. In a scroll in the bottom of the panel are Churchill's words: 'Never in the field of human conflict was so much owed by so many to so few'.

A Lancaster bomber during a Battle of Britain Day. (Photo David. E. Smith)

1. A POTTED BLOG

The statue of warrior queen Boudicca. (Photo Matt Brown)

Medieval graffitti in Norwich Cathedral.

The English Civil War

During the seventeenth century, Norwich was still one of the most important towns in England. It had a thriving marketplace, agricultural land and a textile industry that fed the seaports of Great Yarmouth and King's Lynn, where numerous trading vessels served the Low Countries. Spinners of Dutch, Fleming and Walloon extraction helped ensure that Norwich prospered. They were given the name 'Strangers'. The majority of the Strangers were Protestants fleeing Spanish persecution during the Dutch Rebellion

As Norwich was situated some way away from the main seat of Parliament, there were many issues that meant, when the Civil War broke out, Norwich would in fact back Parliament and not the King who was viewed as tyrannical and incompetent.

In 1628, Parliament had drawn up a petition of rights that had also referred to the Magna Carta, stating that taxes could only be levied by Parliament. King Charles

Norwich Cathedral with Civil War graffiti.

responded by avoiding convening a further parliament for ten years, a period that became known as 'the ten years of tyranny', during which Charles's lack of funds determined his behaviour. The Civil War is discussed later in more depth, but suffice to say, things did not end well for Charles.

The Battle of Trafalgar

This battle is celebrated each year in Norwich by commissioned officers of the Royal Navy in the officers' mess. There is no fixed menu, but the following have been served:

A Parliamentarian trooper, the famed Roundheads. (Photo Paul Chrystal)

STARTERS:
Breaking the Line – smoked salmon and lemon with capers
Cannon Balls – melon balls
Trafalgar Duo – roulade of salmon and sole

MAIN COURSE:
Fleet Broadside – beef Wellington, port wine and shallots
Mizzen Main Course – roast beef and Yorkshire pudding

DESSERT:
Victory Dessert or Dessert Hamilton – poached pears
Hardy's Finale – cheese and biscuits
Coffee
Caribbean and Gibraltar mints

Port is also drunk and passed to the left as stated in the famous quote, 'Do you know the Bishop of Norwich?'
The Loyal Toast (as would be given in Norwich)

This toast to the sovereign was given seated. There are several reasons for this tradition. Charles II, on his return from exile in Holland in May 1660, was on board the *Naseby*, renamed *Royal Charles*. He is reputed to have bumped his head on a low beam in the cabin when responding to a toast. He exclaimed, 'When I get ashore, I'll see that my naval officers run no such risk, for I will allow them from henceforth to remain sitting when drinking my health.'

During the Restoration, the navy received a large influx of gentlemen volunteers who formed a considerable mess. As they were not seamen by upbringing, they would have had great difficulty keeping their feet.

As Prince Regent, George IV, while dining aboard a warship, is reputed to have exclaimed, as the officers rose to drink the king's health, 'Gentlemen, pray be seated. Your loyalty is above suspicion.' The prince was at constant variance with the king and favoured the Whig opposition, but it is a matter of speculation as to where their loyalty was directed. The navy generally considers that loyalty to the person of the sovereign takes procedure over political affiliation.

While he was Duke of Clarence, the future William IV was dining on a man-of-war, where he is also reputed to have bumped his head on a deck beam when he stood up. There are other reasons that are probably more realistic. It was impossible to stand upright 'between decks', except between the beams, so only every third person would have been unable to stand. Also, the table was often fixed to the deck against a settee, so it would have been impossible for half the officers to stand with any degree of dignity. All officers are duty bound to stand if the national anthem is being played during the toast. Officers of the royal yacht also stand as a distinction of the honour of serving on the yacht. In 1966, the Queen extended the privilege to chief and petty officers of the Royal Navy.

In the Royal Navy, there is a set of traditional drinking toasts, employed on different days of the week:

Sunday – Absent friends
Monday – Our ships at sea
Tuesday – Our men
Wednesday – Ourselves
Thursday – A bloody war or a sickly season
Friday – A willing foe and sea room
Saturday – Wives and sweethearts, may they never meet

The Norwich Branch is one of 400 worldwide branches of the Royal Navy Association, which was commissioned in 1979 as a registered charity.

Military Tailoring

The company F. A. Stone & Sons was formed in 1874 and ceased trading in 2011. Founded by Frederick Adolphus Stone, who was a master cutter and tailor to the officers of the 9th and 12th Queen Lancers, he had a great respect for the uniforms of the day. At one stage, one of his sons wanted to introduce civilian wear into the company's range. Frederick was against this but years later he agreed on the proviso that the clothes were kept strictly out of his sight. The company continued with their appointment to fit officers of the Royal Anglian Regiment.

Kitchener's Poster

Even today, when people see the 'Kitchener poster' it is synonymous with a nation of recruiting offices where citizens volunteered do their duty for 'King and Country'. However, it was only after the first wave of volunteers that the poster appeared. In Norfolk, not even 500 men signed up, as most stayed on with the city of Norwich's main employers, the shoe industry.

Kitchener showed disquiet about the poor numbers signing up so he asked Ian Malcolm MP to lead a recruiting drive that was held at St Andrew's Hall, in Norwich. At the same time, the *Eastern Evening News* published a letter from Norwich brewers, Steward & Patteson, stating, that if any of their workers joined the 'New Army', they would have their positions within the company kept open, with further assistance offered to their dependents. That first night of the recruitment saw 250 men sign up, 1,000 the next day and within a week, a further 2,500.

Royal Norfolk Veterans' Association

In 1893 it was decided, via an appeal by Captain A. W. M. Athill, that funds should be raised and put aside for entertainment purposes for the old soldiers of Norwich. As there were monies left over from the appeal, it was agreed that, on 15 January 1894, a dinner would be held for seventy-four veterans at Shirehall Tavern. The good people of Norwich, including mayors and sheriffs, further supported the appeal, resulting in a further sixty-four veterans being fed. A larger venue was sought and, following a meeting in Bethel Street, just before Christmas in

1898, the new venue at the King's Arms pub in Bethel Street was chosen. Captain Athill was chosen as the chairman and part of his duty was to form an association. The Norfolk Veterans' Association was formed, with the following rules:

> To band together in goodwill and the sympathy all discharged soldiers, sailors and marines living in Norfolk who are in possession of medals for active service or long service and good conduct. [Later expanded to include members of the Royal Air Force.]
>
> To provide, if possible, headquarters where meetings can be held, and where information can be obtained with regard to the Association.
>
> To obtain funds for assistance of the most necessitous and deserving cases amongst the members.
>
> To rescue from the workhouse or from a pauper's grave any older soldier, sailor or marine who, through no fault of his own, is reduced to destitution.
>
> To grant pecuniary aid, where necessary, to the widow of a relative of a deceased so that a fitting burial may be provided for him.

The position of president was taken up by Sir E. G. Bulwer KCB, alongside a committee of ten, whose task was to draw up the rules of the association. A 2/- subscription fee was instituted. This followed a public subscription and the dinners continued yearly until the start of the First World War.

The headquarters stayed in Norwich, first in Redwell Street, before moving to Princes Street in 1914. However, because of expensive repairs, a move was needed again, this time to the Old Comrades Club in St Faith's Lane. Due to deterioration, however, another move was required. The association moved to the Keir Hardie Hall, where it has remained since. Veterans carry their King's Colour on all occasions, along with the association standard. The King's Colour dates back to 1914 when it was presented at the Thatched Assembly Rooms.

The position of president was held for many years by the Earl of Leicester, and in 1994, it was taken up by Major A. M. Dicker TD, DL.

As a mark of respect for the regiment that liberated the French city of Blainville-sur-Orne more than seventy years ago, the city's mayor crossed the North Sea to present the Legion d'honneur to some of the veterans. Bill Holden, Ken Mason, Victor Keech and David Johnson were presented with the medal in a moving ceremony at Norwich City Hall, together with the widow of their comrade Jim King.

The honour, an acknowledgement of extraordinary bravery and service in times of war, was created by Napoleon Bonaparte in 1802.

The men, who all took part in the Normandy campaign of the Second World War, continue to be a part of The Royal Norfolk Regiment D-Day Veterans' Association. The event, organized by the association and hosted by the Lord Mayor of Norwich, was attended by families and friends as well as seven French dignitaries, the Sheriff of Norwich, the Norfolk High Sheriff and the Lord Lieutenant of Norfolk.

Lord Mayor of Norwich, Councillor Brenda Arthur, said, 'I'm delighted to host this reception for our veterans, for their bravery and the contribution their actions have made to all our lives. I pay tribute to our veterans for fighting for our liberty, it's a debt we should never forget and we should always be grateful.'

Defence of the Realm Act 1914

The Defence of the Realm Act, or DORA, as it was also known, came into law on 8 August 1914, four days after Britain entered the First World War. The purpose of the act was to give the government extra powers during the war, including censorship. Because of it, many anti-war activists, including Bertrand Russell, were sent to prison. The flying of kites, lighting of bonfires, use of binoculars, feeding wild animals, and talking about military matters were prohibited. Public house opening times were restricted in England until the Licensing Act of 1988 came into force.

During the First World War, the act was amended and extended six times. After the war, parts of DORA were absorbed into the Emergency Powers Act 1920, and at the start of the Second World War, the act was adapted as the Emergency Powers (Defence) Act 1939, which included an act called the Treachery Act 1940, making it a capital offence for assisting the enemy.

The Friendly American Invasion

During the Second World War, East Anglia became home to thousands of US airmen. The United States Eighth Army Air Force arrived in Norfolk in 1942, and between 1942 and 1945 there were, at any one time, around 50,000 US personnel stationed within a thirty-mile radius of Norwich.

The impact of this 'friendly invasion' on local communities was considerable, particularly in villages where American servicemen (and women) vastly outnumbered the local population. Initial suspicion and prejudice towards the Americans rapidly disappeared among those who got to know them. It was a time of jitterbug dances and big-band sounds, and the first taste of peanut butter, chewing gum and Coca-Cola for many Norfolk people. Enduring friendships were forged between the Americans and the local population that still endure today.

The *Eastern Daily Press* printed the following in their edition of 28 September 1942:

In many parts of England the presence of American Soldiers in the streets of our towns and cities has now become a familiar thing ... In the brief off-duty hours when they roam our streets, quiet evidently full of curiosity and interest about the places and the people here in England, one gets an impression, which we could hope is not well-founded, that the degree of friendly contact between them and ourselves has not developed as fully as we all wish to see it ... So far as this area is concerned, the spirit of everyone in East Anglia is one of the heartiest welcome.

In October, a reader wrote to the same newspaper:

Many of us have approached Americans in Norwich and offered them our homes as their homes whilst they are over here, but so far we have had no success. Most of them seem to be looking for something a little more 'peppy' than home life during their first weeks in this country. Moreover, it seems to have been drilled into them very thoroughly that we are a proud people living on the border-line of poverty and starvation, with the result that we can do nothing for them without raiding the baby's money-box or, worse still, his ration card! If you can help us to clear away these misapprehensions and assist us to find some Americans who could appreciate an armchair by the fire, a cup of coffee, a smoke and a talk, we are waiting to open our homes and our hearts to them.

Relations became closer when four squadrons of the Air Training Corps, which included the Norwich wing, paraded in front of the Lord Mayor, the Sheriff and a colonel from the USAAF in October 1942. A cookery class was given, demonstrating to the people of Norwich the history and the relevance of a hamburger, pumpkin cream, Johnny cake and chocolate pin wheels. Christmastime saw up to 400 homes offer American military personnel hospitality, which was arranged by the Lord Mayor's office – 160 men, including ten officers, accepted the offer. The Americans, as a great gesture on Boxing Day, invited sixty ill children from Norwich to join them.

The Bomb Map

In 2007, a Second World War bomb map of Norwich was moved from the Norwich City Engineering Department to the Norfolk Record Office for storage. In 2012, the map, that had originally been put together by the Norwich Air Raid Precautions Department, and which featured 679 paper labels marking the bombs that fell on the city between the years 1940 and 1944, was put on display.

Each label carries the date and the size of the bomb dropped. Due to the age of the map, it was near on impossible for a facsimile to be produced without damaging it. The map is sectioned into three Ordnance Survey maps, 188cm high, 182cm wide and 8cm deep, and placed onto two wooden fibreboards. Metal pins that affixed the labels were corroding due to the way the map had been stored and even some of the pins were showing through the back of the board,

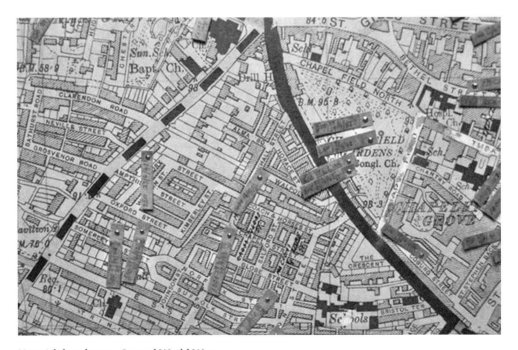

Norwich bomb map, Second World War.

causing a worry for transporting. Around a quarter of the labels and pins were quite damaged and needed to be replaced as a matter of urgency. The remainder showed signs of deterioration through the rest of the paper. To safeguard the map, the deterioration firstly needed to be arrested, the paper labels needed to be stabilized and the backboard needed replacing. It would be time-consuming to remove all 679 labels, but after finding a safe way to do so, the labels and the pins were removed and washed, and the labels pressed and lined with two pieces of Japanese paper. A Tycore support board was used because of its low weight and stability. Japanese heavyweight paper hinges were applied and then the outer strainers were put back together using stainless steel screws. Stainless steel pins coated with Paraloid B-72 replaced the corroded pins. At the back of the board a backing of Plastazote was used to stop the new pins from penetrating the board. An oversized, four-flap enclosure was positioned using a Tyvek sheet. The images were then fully digitalized and made available for the public to view.

National Service

On 27 April 1939, Parliament passed the Military Training Act. This act introduced conscription for men aged 20 and 21, who were then required to undergo six months' military training. At the outbreak of the Second World War, Parliament passed the National Service (Armed Forces) Act, under which all men between 18 and 41 were liable to conscription. It was also announced that single men would be called up before married ones. The registration of all men in each age group began on 21 October starting with those aged 20 to 23. By May 1940, registration had extended only as far as men aged 27, and did not reach those aged 40 until June 1941.

Provision was made in the legislation for people to object to military service on moral grounds. Of the first intake of men aged 20 to 23, an estimated 22 in every 1,000 objected and went before local military tribunals. The tribunals varied greatly in their attitudes towards conscientious objection to military service, as seen by those totally rejected ranging from 6 to 41 per cent.

By the end of 1939, over one and a half million men had been recruited into the armed forces. Of these, 1,128,000 had joined the British Army, with the remainder equally divided between the Royal Navy and the Royal Air Force. Every year from then, twice a month, and once in December because of Christmas, an average of 6,000 young men (over 10,000 at the peak of the Korean War) said their goodbyes and started a new life. Enlistment day was always on a Thursday for the army and air force, and on a Monday for the navy.

For thousands of young men conscripted into the three arms of the defence force, it was their first time away from home, so they all coped with it in their own way. At 18 years of age, young men had to register for service. If you were doing an apprenticeship, or any sort of training for a career, you could opt to defer your service until you were 21.

Private Basil Kybird relates his experiences as a post-war conscript:

January, 1947, one of the coldest winters for many years, snow and ice everywhere, shortages of food and coal. On 16th I had been instructed to report to Britannia Barracks, Norwich. Fortunately, I was living with my parents at 172, Thorpe Road, so it was no hardship for me to find my way walking through the snow. It didn't worry me too much, I was proud to be joining the army and to escape the restraints of Barclays Bank and home life. First, I reported to the guard room. We formed Draft 102 at No. 9 Training Centre and were given an Army number which we had to learn very quickly under threat of terrible consequences. We took with us just essentials such as shaving and washing kit.

We raw recruits were allocated to billets, I to one of the 'spider' huts which held about twelve of us. Next, we were issued with our uniforms and equipment. The Store man, a Sergeant had an uncanny knack of allocating the right sizes although there was the occasional error which caused some amusement! The number of items with which we were issued was incredible: beret, General Issue badge, overcoat, battledress blouse, trousers with button flies (of course), braces, boots, laces, shirts, tie, socks; the outer clothing was all of an itchy, scratchy fabric. Some of these items were in duplicate, then there was a kit bag which eventually had our army number stencilled on it; large and small packs, ammunition pouches, webbing, belt with brass fittings, cape, web anklets, two aluminum mess tins, pint china mug, cutlery, and probably plates were included and I suppose a steel helmet. I had a brass button stick but I think I bought that, as I did tins of boot polish and Dura-Glit. Our uniforms had to have razor-sharp creases and we soon learnt to smear soap along the backs of the creases in our trousers and place them between sheets of cardboard under our mattresses. One thing we had to learn was to wear our berets so the badge was positioned over the left eye.

At some stage, we were issued with identification documents such as the A.B.64 Parts I and II, also dog tags with our name and number impressed on them. We were allocated to platoons I believe named after Royal Norfolk soldiers who had won the Victoria Cross. The beds were metal framed on which we each placed three straw-filled paillasses or 'biscuits' as they were termed, to form mattresses. Lights out was at 11 p.m. whereby the duty sergeant came round to each billet and kindly switched our lights off. It seemed he was round again in no time at all, banging and shouting at 6 a.m. as it was reveille. This was followed by twelve bleary-eyed 'squaddies' rushing to wash, shave, dress and get ready for breakfast. Afterwards was the task of trying to wash greasy plates, cutlery and pint-sized mugs in lukewarm water in outside cauldrons. Not very hygienic but this was the least of our problems.

In the first day or two we were all given a haircut, I can't remember if we paid for it, probably it was only a shilling anyway. We were also instructed in the proper way to lay out our paillasses and kit on our beds. If it wasn't to the Sergeant's satisfaction it was tipped onto the floor and we had to start again.

We were issued with two pairs of boots, complete with hob nails. We were required to acquire a very high gloss on them. This meant many hours of 'boning' to smooth out the grain. To do this first we applied black polish and then used the back of a spoon or similar to gradually wear away the wrinkles. We then used plenty of 'spit and polish' and a damp duster to bring up a high polish on toes and heels. One pair of boots was reserved for parades. Another 'pass-time' was to Blanco our large and small packs, ammunition pouches, belt and webbing. Blanco was a sort of paste stuff which was applied wet then allowed to dry. It came in a variety of shades of khaki depending where we were serving, sometimes white. In the Far East the colour was a dark green, whereas in the Middle East it was a sandy colour.

Britannia Barracks was one of the Army Training Establishments in the country. On enlistment, we were sent to one of these, joining the General Service Corps for initial training. During this time, we were assessed as to in which Regiment or Corps we would serve our King and Country best. Because I could write and had been a bank clerk the Royal Army Ordnance Corps was graced with my presence. Britannia Barracks was the H.Q. of the Royal Norfolk Regiment and was staffed by soldiers of that Regiment who trained us innocents. For many of my colleagues the Army was an unpleasant experience but I enjoyed it, it made me a man out of a toffee-nosed little bank clerk escaping a strict father.

Upon my return to 'civvy' street and Barclays Bank I decided there was something else to life other than figures and consequently joined Norwich City Police. Note Norwich City – my father was still serving in Norfolk Constabulary and I had no wish to be in his grasp!

When my National Service began, 1947 was one of the coldest years in the twentieth century, lasting from January through to March. The country had not recovered from the effects of the war, coal, coke, food all in short supply. In the centre of our hut was a tortoise-shell stove for heating the whole of the hut. We were allowed one bucket of fuel to last twenty-four hours, about enough to fill the stove once! I always liked to have a drink of water handy during the night. I therefore innocently put my pint mug under my bed with water in it. During the night, I went for a drink and nothing came out of my mug: it was frozen solid. I cannot remember how many blankets we were issued with but I found my greatcoat most useful on top. Fortunately, we weren't in the billet much until evening and then there was the NAAFI for a cup of tea and something to eat if we needed it.

We took turns in pairs to do a nightly fire watch patrol. That was a joy! I seemed to click for 4 a.m. to 6 a.m. With a mate Geoff Earle we were instructed to wear gym shoes so in the course of our patrolling we didn't wake anyone up. Can you imagine walking round the whole complex for two hours in the snow wearing plimsolls! The worst of this shift was the extraneous duty of lighting fires outside under cauldrons of water to provide hot water for our mates to shave with and more water for washing up our greasy breakfast things. The hardest part of this exercise was finding dry materials to light the fires with! At some stage during my residence at Britannia Barracks I had a spell of one or two weeks in the garrison hospital with bronchitis, probably as a result.

We must have been issued with singlets and shorts for P.T. and Self-Defence lessons. I remember cross-country runs in the snow, also route marches of about six miles carrying a lot of equipment but I can't remember what. Another frolic in the snow was rifle practice. We had to lie down and fire at targets with .303 Lee-Enfield rifles. Our hands would be frozen to the rifles. Then of course there was bayonet practice. For this we had to charge at suspended sacks of straw, bayonets fixed to our rifles and thrust at the 'enemy' with bloodthirsty shouts.

At least with drill and marching in threes our feet kept warm even if we produced blisters and some had chilblains. It was surprising how many of us had two left feet! Everything was carried out to the count of threes and we soon learned to respond to such commands as 'ef', 'eyet', 'ef', 'eyet', 'ern t eft in frees', 'by th eft ick march', and so on. However, after a bit of 'gentle' coaching from the Drill Sergeant or Sergeant Major, we 'orrible lot' learnt to move as one disciplined body. Rifle drill was another piece of organized chaos, all to the count of three of course, 'loop arms, two three', 'stan at hease, wait forit, wait forit, two three'. It was like learning Mandarin or something equally obscure.

However, in six weeks of basic training we were changed from boys to half-disciplined men in readiness to serve our King and Country. I must mention some of my mates. There was Puggy (Percy) whose father worked on my Uncle Percy's farm. Poor Puggy couldn't read or write. I suppose it was because of family connections that we palled up and I tried to help him along. Unfortunately, his disabilities were discovered and after a couple of weeks he was discharged. Roderick 'Beefy' Boorman was a vicar's son, very sports minded and good at cross-country runs. I believe at the time his father was vicar at Garveston.

Then there was 'Titch', all five feet nothing, from Norwich. I have just remembered another 'comrade in arms', Ray De'ath, who came from the wilds of the countryside south of Norwich. He, Beefy and I had our photos taken at London Street. I still have it among my treasures.

As well as the physical exertions, we had periods in the classroom. One was on Current Affairs. I can't remember what else. Near the end of our six weeks' training, on 20 February, we were assessed as to how we were best suited to serve our King and Country. I believe the Assessment Officer felt that if we could write we were suitable as clerks. It appears the Royal Army Ordnance Corps was short of two clerks so Titch and I were allocated to fill the gap.

2. CALL TO ARMS: PRE-1899

Saxons and Vikings

Just like the Saxons had done before, the Vikings made their way up the River Yare, raiding settlements, and in 866, they invaded East Anglia. This was short lived, as the area of East Anglia soon fell to King Edward the Elder in 917, although many of the Vikings stayed behind. Recent excavations show that a Saxon defence ditch followed the line of St George's Street north of the river. Tombland became the main area, but Vikings continued to wage war, and in 1004 Sweyne came to Norwich with his fleet and razed the whole town.

De Gael's Rebellion, 1075

In 1075, Ralph de Gael rebelled against William the Conqueror. De Gael had at one time been a strong supporter of the king and fought at the Battle of Hastings. By 1069, he was titled Earl of Norfolk, but against the wishes of the king, he married Emma fitz Osbern, daughter of William fitz Osbern, the Earl of Hereford.

The king had been residing in Normandy since 1073. De Gael gathered his troops, and, along with his brother-in-law Roger de Breteuil, 2nd Earl of Hereford and Waltheof, and 1st Earl of Northumberland, began the revolt. However, disaster accompanied it every step of the way. Waltheof very quickly realized in what he had become involved and confessed the conspiracy to

Ralph de Gael, Earl of Norfolk and his wife, Emma, at Norwich Castle, 1070s.

Archbishop of Canterbury, Lanfranc. The archbishop urged de Breteuil to immediately revert his allegiance, excommunicating him and his adherents.

De Breteuil was supposed to bring his force from the west to join his brother-in-law de Gael at the River Severn, along with English Bishop Wulfstan. De Gael was soon met by a royal army led by Bishop Odo of Bayeux and Geoffrey

Gazing wistfully over the ramparts, Emma de Gael besieged at Norwich Castle.

William the Conqueror.

de Montbray, who had orders that all rebels were to have their right foot cut off. The rest of the rebels left Cambridge very quickly, heading towards Norwich, chased by the royal army.

Leaving his wife in charge of Norwich Castle, de Gael tried to broker a deal for support in Denmark, but failed. Emma showed great bravery in resisting the royal forces, before surrendering to Bishop Odo. Ralph did later return to England with a fleet of 200 ships under Cnut Swainson and Earl Halo, but nothing came of it.

Emma and her followers were given forty days to leave Norwich Castle and the realm. She left for her estate in Brittany, where she was joined by her husband.

For his part in the revolt, the king deprived de Gael of his title and all his lands. De Breteuil too had his title and lands removed, but, in addition, he was also sentenced to perpetual imprisonment. It was only after the death of the king that he was released from prison with other political prisoners in 1087. The punishment for Waltheof was somewhat different: on 31 May 1076, he was beheaded at St Giles Hill, Winchester.

The Barons' Rebellion, 1088

When William the Conqueror died in 1087, all his possessions were split between his sons.

His eldest son, Robert, received the title Duke of Normandy, while William, who was known by the nickname 'Rufus', ascended to the English throne. This caused great consternation among the barons, who would have preferred the weaker Robert to have been given the throne. The barons then hatched a plot to have William II replaced, resulting in open fighting breaking out after Easter 1088. The barons were supported by William the Conqueror's half-brothers, Odo of Bayeux and Robert, Count of Mortain. At the same time, Roger Bigold, the new Earl of Norfolk, seized Norwich Castle, which had been the property of the Crown since de Gael's rebellion in 1075.

The barons, however, were not as clever as they thought they were, as they waited in separate castles for reinforcements that were being sent by Robert, Count of Mortain, to arrive from Normandy. This gave William the opportunity to reduce the number of castles owned and run by the barons. Luck also played a part, as the troops from Normandy were forced back by severe storms at sea. Within a short period of time, the king took Rochester Castle in Kent, and the plotters gave up their claim and surrendered. The rebel leaders received leniency from William Rufus, but this was to no avail, as in 1095, a further rebellion, led by the Earl of Northumberland, Robert de Mowbray, took place. In spite of his wife Matilda's valiant defence of Bamburgh Castle, the rebellion was ruthlessly crushed by Rufus. Mowbray was sentenced to life imprisonment at Windsor Castle, while his second in command William of Eu was less fortunately castrated and blinded.

Ethelbert Gate

The gate was built around 1316–17, after the original gate was destroyed during the uprising in August 1272, which had taken place at the Trinity Sunday Tombland Fair after a disagreement between the monks and some citizens. One of the citizens was killed by a priory servant, and a warrant was immediately issued for the arrest of two priory servants. However, Norwich life was far from simple in those days. The monks argued their case, saying that they were exempt from city laws, and they had the doors to Cathedral Close locked. Priory servants attacked passers-by from inside the walls. Together with three barges full of armed men sent from Yarmouth to assist, the priory servants set out from the priory, going on a rampage of the city, looting, burning and attacking citizens as they went – one man was killed.

The following morning, 8 or 9 August, a large number of Norwich citizens mustered in the market place, before marching on the priory. There they set fire to one of the gates to gain access, then went on to torch Cathedral Close and St Ethelbert's Church. The fire spread to other buildings, including the cathedral. The cathedral and the priory were plundered.

Thirteen priory defenders were killed. Prior William de Brunham personally killed one of the assailants. King Henry III, three months before his own death, was forced to intervene. The ailing monarch personally went to Norwich, and, following the trial, at least twenty-nine citizens were hanged.

As part of the damages settlement, Norwich citizens paid for the construction of Ethelbert Gate.

Peasants' Revolt, 1381

The Peasants' Revolt took place in 1381 across large parts of England, fomented by political tensions that stemmed from the effects of the Black Death some forty years earlier and the Hundred Years' War with France that had resulted in high taxes. In Norfolk, the revolt was led by a weaver named Geoffrey Litster, a dyer from the village of Felmingham, and Sir Roger Bacon, a local lord whose family seat was situated in Baconsthorpe. He was also involved with the Suffolk Rebels. Bacon held the poor in high esteem, and by joining forces with Litster, placed his position in jeopardy. Other well-known dignitaries who were forced to side with Litster were Thomas Gyssing, the son of a Norfolk MP, Lord Roger de Scales, Sir Thomas de Morley, Sir John de Brewes, and poll-tax controller, Sir Stephen Hales.

On 14 June, Litster sent out a call to arms for all the rebels in the county. On the 17th, the rebels met in Norwich to talk with Sir Robert Salle, who, being in charge of the city's defence, attempted to negotiate a settlement with the rebels. The townspeople then opened the gates to allow the rebels to enter. In the wake of the rebels' looting, Salle, who was also a war veteran, was pulled from his horse and killed, along with local official Reginald Eccles.

William de Ufford, the Second Earl of Suffolk, fled his estate in disguise to ride to London. Other leading gentry were held by Litster and forced to play the part of household staff. Nobleman and Bishop of Norwich, Henry le Despenser, who was in Stamford, Lincolnshire when the revolt started, marched south with eight men-at-arms and a group of archers. The Bishop's own manor at Hevingham had been plundered and all records burned. Others joined in as le Despenser moved on Norwich. The first major stopover was Peterborough, where le Despenser had many rebels executed. Robert de Gravele cut things fine and escaped death by agreeing, as his head was on the block, to pay those about to execute him eight marks, sixteen pence and twenty-eight cows for his life. The would-be executioners put away their axe and agreed.

The men arrived in Cambridge on 19 June, before heading to Norwich where they arrived on 24 June with many extra men to track down Geoffrey Litster. Villagers from all over the county made a steady path towards Mousehold Heath.

A medieval knight's suit of armour at Norwich Castle.

Led by Sir Roger Bacon, houses of those involved in law and government in Norwich were attacked. Former MP Henry Lominor was robbed of goods worth over one thousand marks. Justice of the Peace Reginald Eccles was taken by the baying mob from his Heigham home, which was then looted. Archdeacon of Norfolk, John de Freton, also had his property looted, along with tax collector Walter de Bixton.

It ended when the rebels were defeated at the Battle of North Walsham on 25 or 26 June. Geoffrey Litster was captured and hanged, drawn and quartered, the execution personally overseen by the Bishop. Henry le Despenser was hailed a hero for quickly ending the East Anglia revolt, but he was deemed to have acted illegally as the executions were without Royal sanction, though this doesn't seem to have had an impact on his career.

Gladman's Insurrection, 1443

Gladman's Insurrection or Rising took place over several days in Norwich in January 1443, characterized by severe riots and disturbances. Not much is known about John Gladman, except that he was a Norwich merchant and a member of the Guild of St George, and a central person in the riots. At one stage during the brouhaha he was dressed as the King of Christmas and his horse was covered in tinsel.

The reason for the riots was due to a power struggle between the merchant class, who were in control of the city government, and the old established church elders, including the cathedral priory (those aggressive priors again) and abbeys. Jurisdiction over certain lands in and around the city was another divisive issue. Several new mills had been built around Norwich, and the abbot of St Benet's claimed that the new mills obstructed the flow of water to his own mills. As a result of this issue, the Earl of Suffolk created an arbitration award in an attempt to settle the dispute between the abbot and the authorities. It required that the city demolish the mills. This would have posed a threat to the city's income and food supply, so the sealing of the award was delayed.

It had been alleged in indictments that, following the riots, the mayor, along with the commonalty, had planned to launch a common insurrection, with arson, plundering and murder on the agenda. A meeting took place in January 1443 to discuss the sealing of the award, when former mayor, Robert Toppes, who had built the Dragon Hall in King Street, removed the common seal from the Guildhall. This action helped fuel the riot.

Medieval combat in the War of the Roses. (Photo Paul Kitchener)

Anger further grew about the power of the church, which manifested itself when a crowd of citizens, including the mayor, placed dry wood against Cathedral Close, while threatening to kill the monks. They also they demanded a change to an agreement made in 1429 about payment of tithes in Carrow. Even the Duke of Norfolk and Earl of Oxford were refused admittance, having been placed in the employ of the king to deal with the riots. This is what then led the city authorities to arrange for John Gladman to ride into the city.

There were no causalities among citizens of the city or the military defending it. The city was fined 3,000 marks, which was later reduced to a thousand. The king assumed control, appointing Sir John Clifton of New Buckenham as Governor of Norwich, for a period of four years until 1447. Charges were brought against the mayor, two sheriffs, eight aldermen, William Hemstede, Robert Toppes and eight others for planning to rise against the bishop and the priors. Other charges were brought against a further ninety-eight people who were with the mayor when he threatened to burn the priory and kill the monks. Five years later, the city declared that John Gladman was a man of sober disposition and a true and faithful servant to God and the king, and that he wasn't the unruly, rebellious thug as portrayed by the clergy.

Battle of Bosworth, 1485

This was the penultimate battle of the War of the Roses, which took place on Monday, 22 August 1485, fought between a Yorkist royal army under King Richard III and a Lancastrian one led by Henry Tudor, Earl of Richmond. The battle resulted in the death of Richard and Henry Tudor's ascension to the throne as Henry VII. Richard III's followers included the Duke of Norfolk and the Earl of Surrey, who, at the time, were in Norwich before being given orders to leave for the Midlands on 16 August. During the campaign, Ambion Hill came under attack from the Duke of Norfolk's archers using fire-arrows. His men then advanced and hand-to-hand fighting ensued. The Duke of Norfolk was killed and his son, Thomas Howard, Earl of Surrey, was wounded and taken prisoner.

Shortly after Richard III was killed, Henry Tudor was acclaimed king. Richard's body was placed on a horse and taken to Leicester, where it was put on display for two days.

Kett's Rebellion, 1549

During the 1540s, England witnessed an increasing crisis in agriculture that led to outbreaks of unrest. The most serious of these was Kett's Rebellion. This all started with the fencing of common lands by landlords for their own use, leaving the common man without land on which to graze his animals. A majority of tenants were forcibly removed from the land by landowners so they could convert arable land into pasture for their own sheep, which became much more profitable with wool being in such high demand.

In July 1549, in a small market town just ten miles outside of Norwich, called Wymondham, there had seen a small disturbance where fences built by the lord of the manor for enclosures were pulled down. The rioters believed that they had the law behind them as Edward Seymour, 1st Duke of Somerset and Lord Protector to Edward VI, had issued a proclamation against illegal enclosures.

A festival took place on the weekend of 6 July, with a play in honour of St Thomas Becket, the co-patron of Wymondham Abbey. The play was illegal, as in 1538 Henry VIII decreed that the name Thomas Becket be removed from the church calendar. On the Monday, a group of men set off to the nearby villages of Morley, St Botolph and Hethersett to tear down fences. Their first target was Sir John Flowerdew, lawyer and landowner from Hethersett who had been agent to Henry VIII as overseer of the demolition of the parish church at Wymondham Abbey. When Flowerdew saw the men tearing down his fences, he bribed them with four pennies to do the same to his enemy, yeoman farmer Robert Kett.

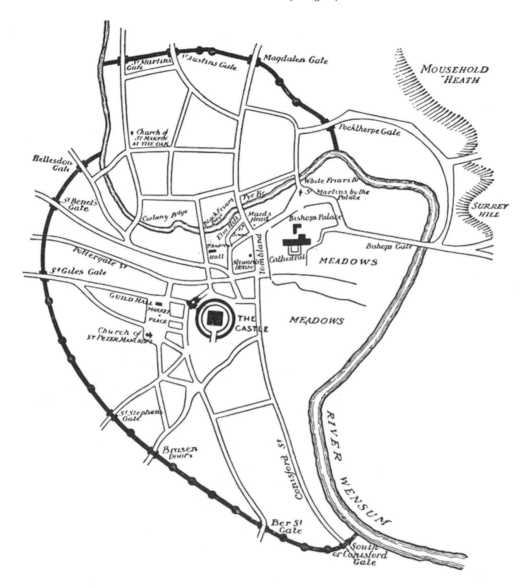

Norwich at the time of Kett's Rebellion, 1540s.

Kett was aged 57, and his family had been farming in the area since the twelfth century. When the rioters turned up at Kett's home, he went out to talk with them, listening while they explained their grievances. It was there and then that Kett decided to join their cause, and helped to tear down his own fences before marching back to the home of Flowerdew.

The following day, the rioters made their way to Norwich, where they were joined by many others, including Kett's brother William. A meeting was convened at the old oak tree on the road from Hethersett to Norwich, known as Kett's Oak, which still stands today.

The next day, the men camped at Bowthorpe, where they were met by the sheriff of Norfolk and Suffolk, Sir Edmund Wyndham. He told them to go home, but they refused. The same happened when mayor of Norwich, Thomas Codd, met them. They were refused permission to enter the city. By Friday, 12 July, they were camped on Mousehold Heath, overlooking the city. Their numbers soon increased to 16,000.

The city authorities contacted London and negotiations took place with the mayor. At that time, former mayor Thomas Aldrich and preacher Robert Watson accepted an invitation to join the rioters. The men then drew up the following

Kett's Oak. (Photo Martin Buro)

lists of twenty-nine grievances, which were signed by Kett, Codd, Aldrich and the representatives of the Hundreds, and sent to Lord Protector Somerset:

1. We pray your grace that where it is enacted for enclosing that it be not hurtful to such as have enclosed saffron grounds for they be greatly chargeable to them, and that from henceforth no man shall enclose any more.

2. We certify your grace that whereas the lords of the manors have been charged with certain free rent, the same lords have sought means to charge the freeholders to pay the same rent, contrary to right.

3. We pray your grace that no lord of no manor shall common upon the common.

4. We pray that priests from henceforth shall purchase no lands neither free nor bond, and the lands that they have in possession may be letten to temporal men, as they were in the first year of the reign of King Henry VII.

5. We pray that all the marshes that are held of the king's majesty by free rent or of any other, may be at such price as they were in the first year of King Henry VII.

6. We pray that reed ground and meadow ground may be at such price as they were in the first year of King Henry VII.

7. We pray that all bushels within your realm be of one stice, that is to say, to be in measure VIII gallons.

8. We pray that priests or vicars that be not able to preach and set forth the word of God to his parishioners may be thereby put from his benefice, and the parishioners there to choose another or else patron or lord of the town.

9. We pray that the payments of castle ward rent, blanch farm, and office lands, which hath been accustomed to be gathered of the tenements, whereas we suppose the lords ought to pay the same to their bailiffs for their rents gathering, and not the tenants.

10. We pray that no man under the degree of a knight or esquire keep a dove house, except it hath been of an old ancient custom.

11. We pray that all freeholders and copyholders may take the profits of all commons, and there to common, and the lords not to common nor take profits of the same.

12. We pray that no feodary within your shores shall be a counsellor to any man in his office making, whereby the king may be truly served, so that a man being of good conscience may be yearly chosen to the same office by the commons of the same shire.

13. We pray your grace to take all liberty of leet your own hands whereby all men may quietly enjoy their commons with all profits.

14. We pray that copyhold land that is unreasonable rented may go as it did in the first year of King Henry VII. And that at the death of a tenant, or of a sale the same lands to be charged with an easy fine as a capon or a reasonable sum of money for a remembrance.

15. We pray that no priest shall hold no other office to any man of honour or worship, but only to be resident upon their benefices, whereby their parishioners may be instructed within the laws of God.

16. We pray that all bond men may be made free, for God made all free with his precious blood shedding.

17. We pray that Rivers may be free and common to all men for fishing and passage.

18. We pray that no man shall be put by your Feudatory to find any office, unless he holdeth of your grace in chief, or capite [tenure] above 10 by year.

19. We pray that the poor mariners or fishermen may have the whole profits of their fishings such as porpoises, grampuses, whales, or any great fish so it be not prejudicial to your grace.

20. We pray that every proprietary parson or vicar having a benefice of 10 or more by year, shall either by themselves, or by some other person teach poor men's children of their parish the book called the catechism and the primer.

21. We pray that it be not lawful to the lords of any manor to purchase lands freely [that are freehold], and to let them out again by copy or court roll to their great advancement, and to the undoing of your poor subjects.

22. We pray that no proprietary parson or vicar, in consideration of avoiding trouble and lawsuit between them and their poor parishioners, which they daily do proceed and attempt, shall from henceforth take for the full contents of all the tenths which now they do receive, but 8.

23. We pray that no lord, knight, esquire, nor gentlemen do graze nor feed any bullocks or sheep if he may spend forty pounds a year by his lands but only for the provision of his house.

24. We pray that no man under the degree of [word missing] shall keep any conies [rabbits] upon any freehold or copyhold unless he pale them in so that it shall not be to the commons' annoyance.

25. We pray that no person of what estate degree or condition he be shall from henceforth sell the award ship of any child, but that the same child if he

live to his full age shall be at his own choosing concerning his marriage the King's wards only except.

26. We pray that no manner of person having a manor of his own, shall be no other lord's bailiff but only his own.

27. We pray that no lord, knight, or gentleman shall have or take in form any spiritual promotion.

28. We pray your grace to give licence and authority by your gracious commission under your great seal to such commissioners as your poor commons have chosen, or to as many of them as your majesty and your counsel shall appoint and think meet, for to redress and reform all such good laws, statues, proclamations and all other your proceedings; which hath been hidden by your Justices of your peace, Sheriff, Feudatories, and other your officers, from your poor commons, since the first year of the reign of your noble grandfather King Henry VII.

29. We pray that those your officers, which have offended your grace and your commons, and [are] so proved by the complaint of your poor commons, do give unto these poor men so assembled 4d. every day so long as they have remained there.

On 21 July, a messenger from the King's Council arrived in Norwich, where, together with city officials, they went to Mousehold Heath to offer the men a pardon. This was refused, as they claimed that no person within the group had committed treason. The gates of the city were then shut and the men declared rebels. Kett had to feed his men, but with the city gates firmly shut, he was left with no other alternative other than to attack the city.

At Bishopgate Bridge on the evening of 21 July, the rebels started taking control of the city. The King's herald tried in vain to stop the rebels, and had to flee, fearing for his life. By return, the king sent the Marquess of Northampton with 1,500 men and a contingent of Italian mercenaries to end the rebellion. When he arrived at the city, the marquess sent his herald to demand that the city be returned. Deputy Mayor Augustine Steward sent communication back, stating that the rebels had retired to the safety of Mousehold Heath.

On 31 July, the royal army began patrolling the Tombland area, unaware of the rebels hiding in the alleys. The rebels launched a hit-and-run attack on the troops. Street battles continued through to the early hours of the next morning. Lord Edmund Sheffield was placed in command of a unit of the royal army to find the rebels who had been seen on the cathedral precinct, at St Martin-at-Palace and Bishopgate by the Great Hospital. It was by St Martin-at-Palace that Lord Sheffield fell from his horse into a ditch. He quickly removed his helmet so that the rebels would see who he was and take him prisoner. This made not a jot of difference and a rebel by the name of Fulke struck Sheffield on the head, killing him. After his death, Northampton ordered his men to retreat. They then made their way to Cambridge.

The king then sent a much stronger army led by the Earl of Warwick, of 14,000 men, including mercenaries from Germany and Spain. Although pardons were offered, the rebels stayed loyal to Kett. Consequently, the battles continued and the city stayed under rebel control.

The Earl of Warwick forcibly entered the city on 24 August by attacking the rebels at St Stephen's and Brazen gates. For some reason, Warwick's baggage train got lost and ended up in Bishopgate where it fell into the hands of the rebels. A group of soldiers led by Captain Drury then went to retrieve it, as, crucially, it consisted of several artillery pieces. They broke down the city walls near Magdalen and Pockthorpe gates. Warwick's army launched their counter-attack and street fighting continued throughout the day and into the night.

On 26 August, a further 1,500 foreign mercenaries entered the city, which meant that it was now no longer safe for the rebels to remain on Mousehold Heath. So, they went underground to prepare for the looming street showdown.

On the morning of 27 August, Dussindale became the site of the final battle. Totally exhausted from the previous days' fighting, many rebels were killed, while others fled for their lives. It is not known for sure where Dussindale was, but it is believed to have been part of Mousehold into the Long Valley, in the area of what is now Gertrude Road and its allotments.

It is thought that up to 3,000 rebels were killed at the final battle, with the royal army losing only 250 men. The next morning, the rebels that were caught were hanged at the Oak of Reformation and outside Magdalen Gate. It's hard to put a figure on how many were hanged, but it is believed to be anywhere between thirty and 300.

Robert Kett was captured at the village of Swanington and taken with his brother William to the Tower of London. They were both found guilty of treason and were sentenced to be hanged, drawn and quartered. However, this was changed and the Ketts were taken back to Norwich in December, where they were held in the Guildhall. On 7 December, Robert Kett was hanged from the walls of Norwich Castle. On the same day, the same fate befell William at Wymondham Abbey.

The following year, the city of Norwich declared that 27 August would be a holiday to commemorate the deliverance of the city from Kett's Rebellion. The annual holiday continued to be celebrated for over a century.

In 1948, former mayor Alderman Fred Henderson, who had been imprisoned in the castle for his role in the food riots of 1885, proposed that a statue of Robert Kett be erected in the city. Instead, a wall plaque was placed on the walls of the castle, using Henderson's wording. The plaque was unveiled in 1949, 400 years after the rebellion.

The Civil War, 1642–51

The people of Norwich enjoyed a prosperous way of life during the seventeenth century, as the city remained a very important part of England. When the Civil War broke out, numerous issues meant that the people of Norwich would support Parliament and not King Charles I. What most townspeople questioned was the 'Divine right of Kings'. What had caused such an abuse of power by the king? Why had it become necessary to stand up to a king who, in the eyes of Norwich, had proved himself to be a tyrannical and incompetent ruler?

All over England, the question was debated, as the king introduced many unpopular laws, such as the collection of taxes. At this time, Parliament was but an advisory body when called on by the king. The body was subject to dissolution if and when the king found it fit to do so.

Parliament was made up of the gentry, who took full responsibility for the collection of taxes. Whilst the king's support of the French Huguenots was very popular in Parliament, his marriage to the Catholic Henrietta-Marie de Bourbon was afforded less enthusiasm. Foreign matters drained the Crown's fiscus, so he decided to raise taxes.

In 1628, Parliament drew up the Petition of Rights, declaring that the raising of taxes could only be enacted through Parliament. Following this, the king avoided convening another parliament for ten years, a period which became known as 'Ten years of Tyranny'. To raise funds, the king introduced a levy on the inland counties to fund a royal navy. He also formulated a new policy of introducing fines for petty offences.

Norwich was considerably affected by this. In 1635, the county of Norfolk was ordered to pay £8,000, which included £1,100 from Norwich to go towards the upkeep of the royal navy. More funds were demanded in 1637, 1638 and 1640. The local authorities met in secret to discuss the legality of the monarch's demands and ways of sourcing such amounts of money. For those who protested and lost their cases in court, further fines were levied.

The king had shown that he had strong beliefs in High Anglicanism, but the Puritans accused the king of finding a way to reintroduce Catholicism to England. In Norwich, a small group of concerned Puritans complained to Matthew Wren, the Bishop of Norwich. The bishop had already caused a great deal of offence with his twenty-eight articles that required communion tables in every church to stand close to the east wall of the chancel. To the Puritans, this was a return to everything that was pre-Reformation Church.

When a rebellion took place in Scotland, the king went to Parliament to ask for funds. However, he was forced to hear that laws had been drawn up that stopped him from imposing taxes and dissolving Parliament without their consent.

In 1642, Charles, accompanied by 400 royal troops, arrived at Parliament to arrest five members for treason. The speaker of the house refused to state where the men were. As he had lost all his powers, the king moved with his family to York, leaving Parliament in charge at Westminster.

Due to the fact that Norwich had a strong Puritan community, it became a supporter of Parliament. During the month of December 1642, Parliament decreed that the counties of Norfolk, Suffolk, Essex, Cambridgeshire, Hertfordshire, the Isle of Ely and the county city of Norwich would join together for mutual aid, defence and preservation, to be known as the 'Eastern Association'.

Norwich went on to offer men and other resources to the Parliamentarian war effort, but parts of the city still supported the Crown. When Charles was defeated and incarcerated, Royalist factions within the city fomented strife during the Second Civil War of 1648/9. Tensions culminated in the 'Great Blow' of 1648, when the houses of leading Puritans and that of Sheriff Thomas Ashwell were attacked. Troops were called in to stop the rioting, which had spread to St Stephen's Street. During this time, barrels of gunpowder that had been stored at the Royalist Committee house, exploded on Bethel Street, killing dozens.

Grain Revolt, 1766

As grain became scarce and more expensive, local businessmen were blamed for profiteering. Dissatisfaction boiled over when a mob came to the city and started to attack mills, and a house in Tombland that was used as a bakery. Army dragoons were ready to ride in from Colchester, while Mayor John Patteson bravely took his life into his own hands when he decided to read out the Riot

Act. He called for loyal citizens to help, and, armed with clubs, they broke up the troubles without the need for the military.

The Luddite Rebellion, 1811–16

In a report dated 18 May 1816, Norwich magistrate John Patteson updated the Home Office on riots in the city:

My Lord,

Mr Yallop, our worthy Mayor, had the honour of writing to your Lordship yesterday, to express to you that the Barrack Master had received the West Norfolk Regt. of [Militia] under the command of Lt. Coll. Nelthorp into the Barrack, & also to request to your Lordship that that Regt. should not be disbanded next week as proposed. The magistrates are anxious to impress this request upon your Ldships mind, as well that they may avail themselves of that force so ably commanded, as to prevent the return at this moment of many men of that regiment to their families in this City. It cannot be denied but that the manufacturing employment here is very low, which with the daily increasing price of flour & bread causes a general irritation in the minds of the labouring poor & the class immediately above them.

Early yesterday the magistrates issued the enclosed handbill – they met at their hall about 7 o' Clock the people began to collect together – at ½ past 8 they were in considerable numbers, when the Magistrates thought proper to address them on their unusual appearances, stating to their them the necessity they should be made of reading the Riot act if they did not disperse – some of the Norwich Light Horse Volunteers having passed through the Market to the Swan Inn their place of rendezvous, the mob following them – a person from that Inn soon came to the hall to give notice of their breaking windows and committing other outrages – upon which about ¼ before 9 o' Clock the Riot act was read in due form.

About 15 of the Royal Dragoons, all there were in the barracks, under the command of Capt. Phipps, then came into the market & were joined by 29 in the Norwich Light Horse Volunteers under the command of Capt. Hudson – more of that corps could not be collected as many of them reside at some distance from the City. A Captain's guard from the West Norfolk [Militia] was placed in the Town Hall. All exerted themselves to the utmost & came assisted by a considerable number of respectable inhabitants, so that the market place was soon cleared & the people assembled their dispersed. Several persons were taken into custody & at this moment the Mayor & Magistrates employed in enquiring into their offences. It is very certain the people came into the market with a riotous determination having their pockets filled with Stones & offensive weapons. There is every reason to suspect they will renew their attempt this evening – every necessary precaution will be taken the propriety of which is more apparent every moment, from information we receive, that the people did not expect the Magistrate to have been in such a state of preparation last night to meet any attempt to disturb the peace of the City – their object will never be absent from our minds, nor will any exertion be omitted on the part of the Military, the Magistrates & a large number of respectable inhabitants to insure it.

I have now to apologize for addressing your Lordship, which I do at the request of the Mayor Mr Yallop, whose attention is altogether employed in hearing the various reports which are brought to him & in giving the necessary directions.

I can assure your lordship no man could fill the office better, nor greater Zeal in satisfying its duties – I have requested his signature to this letter to give it all the official Sanction your Lordship may wish.

I have etc.

John Patteson

The Mayor has blotted out his Signature out of delicacy to the signing of his own promises.

Napoleonic Wars

In June 1808, the 9th (East Norfolk) Regiment of Foot sailed for Portugal for service in the Peninsular War. In August, it saw action at the Battle of Roliça and the Battle of Vimeiro. A year later, the regiment participated in the Walcheren expedition to the Netherlands.

After returning to the Peninsula in 1810, the regiment, saw action at the battles of Bussaco Sabugal and Fuentes de Oñoro.

In 1812, the regiment saw action at the Siege of Ciudad Rodrigo, the Siege of Badajoz, the Battle of Salamanca, and the Siege of Burgos.

In 1813, it saw action in the Battle of Vitoria and at the Siege of San Sebastián, and then fought the French army in France at the battles of Nivelle and the Nive.

Soon afterwards, the regiment found itself in Canada, joining most of the Duke of Wellington's veterans to help stop an invasion by the Americans. It was

The inside of a British infantry officer's shako during the Napoleonic Wars. It reads: 'TOMLINSON, *HATTER*, Back of the Inns. NORWICH.'

too late for the Battle of Waterloo, but the 1st Battalion was part in the Army of Occupation in France. The 2nd Battalion was disbanded at the end of 1815.

The Captain Swing Riots, 1830

The Swing Riots were a series of disturbances that started in Kent. One of the main demands was for a wage increase. Another was for the use of threshing machines to be stopped. The ringleaders went on to use arson to achieve their demands. Some farmers supported their employees, as they saw the increasing of wages as a form of forcing the Church to abolish the tithe system.

Captain Swing did not exist – swing was used in reference to the swing of the flail in the threshing process – the name was only used on letters of demand from farmers. Taking its name from a mythical Captain Swing, the riots quickly spread all over southern England. The ringleader was 48-year-old gardener Robert West, an ex-soldier from the Napoleonic Wars.

On Saturday, 27 November 1830, up to 200 rioters came to the paper mills situated at Taverham and Lying. A proprietor, William Johnson of Lyng Mill, took on extra men to prevent his machines from being attacked. West denied being the ringleader, but did admit that, once inside the mill, he worked like a 'good un' in a rampage of destruction. Witnesses, however, were adamant that he was the ringleader. Further raids took place in the afternoon, and, once again, eyewitnesses claimed that West was the ringleader. Although machinery was destroyed, no other damage was done and no one was hurt in any way. There was considerable sympathy for the rioters in Norwich. An urgent message from the mill owners was sent to Norwich, whence a detachment of 1st Dragoon Guards was sent. When they arrived at Taverham, most of the rioters had already left. The other rioters had made their way to Lyng, unaware that they were being watched. Robert West was seized while the cries of 'there goes old Bob' could be heard.

Riots took place just outside of Norwich on the evening of 29/30 November 1830. A threshing machine owned by William Brett of Burton Overy was destroyed. Riots also took place at East Tuddenham, where Jane Taylor was put on trial. Farmer Lee Amis from Rougham who owned ten acres of land, went with other labourers to another farm to demand a rise in wages. Reverend Thomas Elliston of Haddiscoe was attacked at the Crown Inn when he went to receive his tithe. After refusing to reduce his tithe, he was locked in a room until he agreed to the demands of the crowd.

Richard Knockolds, a labourer from Swanton Abbot, set fire to a haystack in January 1831. A 'Swing' letter was sent to J. Deary, which read, 'J Deary mind your yards be not of a fire dam you. D'. Government response to the riots was harsh: across the country nineteen ringleaders were hanged and over 500 were sentenced to transportation, including West who never saw his wife and children again.

Afghan and Sikh Wars

The 9th (East Norfolk) Regiment saw action in Kabul in August 1842, in what was the First Anglo-Afghan War, and at the battles of Mudki and Ferozeshah, the latter at Christmas 1845. In February 1846, the regiment went on to participate in the Battle of Sobraon in the First Anglo-Sikh War. In 1853, The Norfolk Artillery Militia was formed.

3. CALL TO ARMS: POST 1899

Anglo-Boer War, 1899–1902

The Norfolk Regiment saw its first action at the Battle of Poplar Grove in March 1900 en route to invade the Transvaal, before taking part in the capture of Johannesburg on 31 May 1900. From June 1900 until the end of hostilities the regiment was involved in counter-insurgency operations against Boer guerrillas in the Cape Colony, the Orange Free State and the Transvaal, as well as conducting garrison duties, principally in Rustenburg in the Western Transvaal.

First World War, 1914–18

The Norfolk Regiment raised nineteen battalions, was awarded seventy battle honours and one Victoria Cross and lost some 6,000 men during the course of the war.

Yeomanry at Maid's Head Hotel, during the Boer War, 1900.

This knife from the Boer War is engraved 'P LARSON NORWICH'.

At the outbreak of the First World War, the Norfolk Regiment, which comprised three regular and three territorial battalions, was expanded five-fold. With the alarming casualty rate of the war, soldiers from areas such as London and Essex joined the regiment. Equally, soldiers from Norfolk also ended up in regiments all over the country.

A man wishing to join the army could do so, providing that he passed certain physical tests and was willing to enlist for a number of years. The recruit had to be taller than 5ft 3in. and aged between 18 and 38, although he could not be sent overseas until he was 19. He would join at the regimental depot, or at one of its recruiting offices. The man had a choice over the regiment to which he wished to be posted. He would typically join the army for a period of seven years' full-time service, followed by another five in the army reserves. These terms were for infantry; the other arms had slightly different ones. For example, in the artillery it was for six years plus six in the reserves.

When war was declared, there were 350,000 former soldiers in the Army Reserve, ready to be called back to fill the strengths of their regiments.

Throughout the war, it was still possible to enlist into the regular army on standard terms, usually for the twelve years described above. In addition to this, on Lord Kitchener's instructions in August 1914, a new form of 'short service' was introduced, under which a man could serve for 'three years or the duration of the war, whichever the longer'. Men joining on this basis, including all of 'Kitchener's New Army' and the 'Pals' units, were technically of the regular army and were serving on like terms.

The wartime volunteers continued to have, in theory at least, a choice as to the regiment they wished to join. They had to meet the same physical criteria as the peacetime regulars, but men who had previously served in the army would now be accepted up to the age of 45. There are many recorded instances of underage, and indeed overage, men being accepted into the services. It was not necessary to produce evidence of age or even of one's name in order to enlist.

Enlistment into the Territorial Force, or TF, remained open. The TF was mobilized in August 1914, its men on full-time 'embodied' service. Men joining from September 1914 were expected to sign the 'Imperial Service Obligation', which gave the army powers to send them overseas or transfer them to a different TF unit if required.

By the spring of 1915, it had become clear that voluntary recruitment was not going to provide the numbers of men required for the continued prosecution of the expanding war. Under the Derby Scheme, the government passed the National Registration Act 1915 that required all men and women, between the ages of 15 and 65 years of age, to register their name and residential location on 15 August 1915. This served as a step towards stimulating recruitment and to discover how many men between the ages of 15 and 65 were engaged in which trade. The results of this census became available by mid-September.

Disappointed with the results of the Derby Scheme, the government introduced the Military Service Act 1916 on 27 January. Voluntary enlistment was stopped, and all British males were now deemed to have enlisted on 2 March 1916, that is, they were conscripted if they were aged between 19 and 41, and resided in Great Britain (excluding Ireland) and were unmarried or a widower as at 2 November 1915. Conscripted men were no longer given a choice of which service, regiment or unit they wished to join, although if a man preferred the navy, it got priority to receive him. On 25 May 1916, the act was extended to include married men, and the lower age dropped to 18. This was not the first time in British history that there had been compulsory military service, but it was the first time that it was universally applied.

Although most of us primarily think of the Great War in terms of life and death in the trenches, only a relatively small proportion of the army actually served in them. The trenches were the front lines – the most dangerous places. Behind them, there was a mass of supply lines, training establishments, stores, workshops, headquarters and all the other elements of the 1914–1918 system of war, in which the majority of troops were employed. The trenches were the domain of the infantry, with the supporting mortars and machine-gun teams, the engineers, the medics, and the forward positions of the artillery observers.

The type and nature of the trench positions varied a lot, depending on the local conditions. For example, in the area of the River Somme in France, the ground is chalky and is easily dug. The trench sides would crumble after rain, so would be built up – revetted – with wood, sandbags or any other suitable material. At Ypres in Belgium, the ground is naturally boggy and the water table very high, so trenches were not really dug, but more built up using sandbags and wood, in the manner of breastworks. In parts of Italy, trenches were dug in rock; in Palestine in desert. In France, the trenches ran through towns and villages, through industrial works, coalmines, brickyards, across railway tracks, through farms, fields and woods, across rivers, and canals and streams. Each feature presented its own set of challenges for the men who had to dig in and defend. In the major offensives of 1915, 1916 and 1917, many trench positions were only held for a few days at a time before the next advance moved them on, into what had been no man's land, or the enemy position. These trenches were scratch affairs, created as the advancing troops dug in, and were sometimes little more than 18 inches deep.

Trench conditions varied widely between different theatres of war, different sectors within a theatre, and with the time of year and the weather. Trench life was, however, always one of considerable squalor, with so many men living in a very restricted space. Scraps of discarded food, empty tins and other waste, the

New recruits leaving Thorpe Station (Norwich Station), 1914.

The Norwich market place, 1914. The Lee-Enfield rifles are stacked in the age-old manner that pre-dates the Napoleonic Wars.

Jovial troops departing Thorpe Station (Norwich Station), blissfully unaware of the Western Front 'meat grinder' that awaits them.

Norwich, the Great War: a military gymnastics team poses impressively.

nearby presence of the latrine, the general dirt of living half underground, and not being able to wash or change for days or weeks at a time created conditions of severe health risk – and that is not counting the military risks. Vermin, including rats and lice were numerous. Disease was spread by both them and by the maggots and flies that thrived on the nearby remains of decomposing human and animal corpses. Troops in the trenches were also subjected to the weather: the winter of 1916/17 in France and Flanders was the coldest in living memory. The trenches flooded sometimes to waist height, whenever it rained. Men suffered from exposure, frostbite, and many diseases brought on or made worse by living in such a way. Trench foot, a wasting disease of the flesh caused by the foot being wet and cold while confined in boots and puttees for days on end, crippled countless thousands of troops.

The maintenance of discipline in the army has always been considered a very serious affair. Whilst it is clear from statistics that there was much ill-discipline in the army throughout the war, most of it was of a non-serious nature. The instances of failure to obey orders were relatively few, and the number of men convicted and subjected to serious punishment was miniscule as a proportion of the whole. The disciplinary regulations outlined here were defined by the Army Act and the Field Service Regulations.

Small-scale misdemeanours included everything from matters of individual presentation such as being unshaven and untidy to losing kit, not saluting or addressing superiors correctly, dirty or incorrect equipment, being late on parade or after curfew, etc. These would be detected and dealt with by the NCOs and officers of a man's own unit. NCOs often gave men extra fatigues or exercise as punishment for small matters. Being confined to barracks or losing a day's pay was a torment too, for men who were eager for rest and amusement.

For moderately serious crimes, a man could elect to be tried by a district court martial, or be convicted and sentenced by his commanding officer, or CO. The CO could sanction maximum punishments such as detention up to 28 days, field punishment up to 28 days, forfeit of all pay up to 28 days, and for drunkenness, a fine up to 10 shillings. The CO could impose minor punishments, with the offender having no right to a court martial, including confinement to camp for up to 14 days, extra guard duty, a reprimand, severe reprimand or admonition.

Serious matters were tried by courts martial. Some of these offences were ones that would have been tried by a civilian court if the man had not been on active service, for example murder or rape. Other offences were purely military in nature, such as desertion.

Offences tried and corresponding penalties handed down by courts martial included:

Shamefully delivering up a garrison to the enemy – death
Shamefully casting away arms in the presence of the enemy – death
Misbehaving before the enemy in such a manner as to show cowardice – death
Leaving the ranks on pretence of taking wounded men to the rear – penal servitude
Wilfully destroying property without orders – penal servitude
Leaving his CO to go in search of plunder – death
Forcing a safeguard – death
Forcing a soldier when acting as sentinel – death
Doing violence to a person bringing provisions to the forces – death
Committing an offence against the person of a resident in the country in which he was serving – death
Breaking into a house in search of plunder – death
By discharging firearms intentionally occasioning false alarms on the march – death
When acting as a sentinel on active service sleeping at his post – death
By discharging firearms negligently occasioning false alarms in camp – cashiering or imprisonment
Causing a mutiny in the forces, or endeavouring to persuade persons in HM forces to join in a mutiny – death
Striking his superior officer – death
Offering violence or using threatening language to his superior officer – penal servitude
Disobeying in such a manner as to show a wilful defiance of authority, a lawful command given personally by his superior officer – death
Disobeying a lawful command given by his superior officer – penal servitude
When concerned in a quarrel, refusing to obey an officer who ordered him into arrest – cashiering
Striking a person in whose custody he was placed – cashiering or imprisonment
Deserting HM service, or attempting to desert – death
Fraudulent enlistment, first offence imprisonment, second – penal servitude

Assisting a person subject to military law to desert – imprisonment

Behaving in a scandalous manner unbecoming the character of an officer and a gentleman – cashiering

When charged with the care of public money, embezzling the same – penal servitude

When charged with the care of public goods, misapplying the same [applicable to quartermasters] – penal servitude

Wilfully maiming himself with intent to render himself unfit for service – imprisonment

Drunkenness – cashiering or imprisonment

Committing the offence of murder – death

Serving in Ireland at the start of the war, the 1st Battalion of the Norfolks was given orders to mobilize on 4 August, which was the day that Britain declared war on Germany. Part of the 15th Brigade, 5th Division, the battalion left Belfast for France 14 August to become part of the British Expeditionary Force (BEF), which first saw action against the German army at the Battle of Mons in August 1914.

The 2nd Battalion was serving in Bombay, India, in the 18th Brigade, part of the 6th (Poona) Division, of the British Indian Army when the war started. The 2nd Battalion of the Norfolks fought in the Mesopotamian campaign. The way the prisoners were treated by a callous enemy after the fall of Kut al Amara in April 1916, mirrors what would later befall the Royal Norfolks in the Far East during the Second World War.

There were two territorial force battalions, the 4th and 5th. They were part of the Norfolk and Suffolk Brigade, East Anglian Division. In May 1915, these became the 163rd (Norfolk and Suffolk) Brigade, 54th (East Anglian) Division. The two territorial battalions went on to serve in the Gallipoli campaign in mid-1915. The 1/5th included men recruited from the royal estate at Sandringham.

On 12 August 1915, the 1/5th Battalion suffered heavy losses at Gallipoli after becoming isolated during an attack. Gallipoli tends to be associated with the heroic bravery and sacrifice of the ANZACs. British (and French) casualties in reality exceeded those of the Australians and New Zealanders.

The Second Battle of Gaza in 1917 saw the 1/4th and 1/5th battalions suffer 75 per cent casualties, which amounted to 1,100 men. The 1/6th (Cyclist) Battalion was stationed in Norwich at the outbreak of the war, but the 1/6th was not deployed overseas, remaining in Norfolk until 1918 when it was sent to Ireland.

The 2/4th and 2/5th battalions were both raised in September 1914, drawing from the few men of the 4th and 5th battalions who did not volunteer for imperial service overseas. This meant that the territorial units were split into first-line units, which were liable to be sent overseas, while the second-line units were intended to act as a reserve at home.

The Norfolk Yeomanry, which saw action at the Gallipoli, were moved to Egypt, where they were reorganized as infantry and retitled the 12th (Norfolk Yeomanry) Battalion, Norfolk Regiment, in the 74th (Yeomanry) Division, also known as the 'Broken Spur' division.

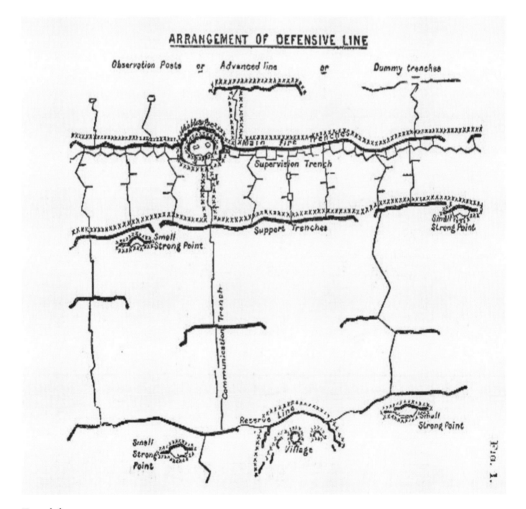

Trench layout.

In 1917, the battalion went on to fight in the Palestine theatre at the Third Battle of Gaza, also known as the battles of Beersheba and Nebi Samwil. It was then involved in the Tell 'Asur campaign of March 1918. The 74th Division was then sent to join forces with the Allied forces on the Western Front, where the 12th Norfolks were attached to the 31st Division, serving in the Hundred Days' Offensive.

On 1 July 1916, the first day of the Somme Offensive, the 8th (Service) Battalion, Norfolk Regiment, part of the 18th Division, was deployed at Carnoy in the extreme south of the British sector. As was the case with almost all the British troops that day, the Norfolks suffered dreadfully, with 334 casualties, including 105 killed. Several players from Norwich City FC took part in the offensive, including manager Major Franklin Charles Buckley who was seriously wounded. George and Margaret Hindley of 31 Ashby Street, Norwich lost two sons on that first day, in the attack between Montauban and Mametz.

One in three Norfolk men joined the forces, estimated to have been around 100,000. They joined different regiments and units all over the country. Of this number, 12,000 Norfolk men lost their lives, of which 6,000 alone were from the Norfolk Regiment.

Great War Memorial Cottages road sign.

The Norfolk Regiment War Memorial with a glimpse of the Memorial cottages in the background.

Above left: Preparing for a gas attack, Western Front. (Photo Otis Historical Archives)

Above right: Tommies shifting a heavy mobile forge, Western Front, 1918. (Photo National Library of Scotland)

Below: Good friends. A Royal Artillery driver takes times out, as does his horse. (Photo National Library of Scotland)

The regiment had built memorial cottages next to Mousehold Heath to commemorate the soldiers of the regiment who had died. Disabled soldiers and their families were housed in them. This was continued after the Second World War, when bungalows were built in Norwich for the same purpose. (Today these memorial cottages change hands on the open market, a recent sale of one fetching £360,000, which is probably well beyond your average squaddie's budget.)

During the First World War, the Norfolk Yeomanry was awarded the battle honours Ypres 1918, France and Flanders 1918, Gallipoli 1915, Egypt 1915–17, Gaza, Jerusalem, Tell 'Asur Palestine 1917–18.

In 2009, it was reported that soldiers from Norwich killed in one of the bloodiest battles of the First World War, would be reburied with full military honours after having been exhumed from mass graves, together with others from Suffolk. The remains of servicemen from Britain and Australia, killed during the Battle of Fromelles, were discovered in northern France in 2007. It was confirmed by the Ministry of Defence that the reburials would take place in 2010, close to the original burial site named Fromelles (Pheasant Wood) Military Cemetery. Sergeant Robert Chaplin, aged 19, and Lance Sergeant Alan Shreeve, aged 23, both from Norwich, were among those that were reinterred. The battle took place on 19 July 1916, the first major battle on the Western Front to involve Australian troops. The British divisions lost 1,547 men and the Australian divisions, 5,533.

Second World War, 1939–45

Prior to the start of the Second World War, the Air Ministry's specification F.9/35 called for a two-seat four-gun turret fighter. The pilot was to sit the front, while a gunner occupied the rear with a swinging turret. The Defiant was built by a Norwich company, Boulton Paul Aircraft Limited, which had acquired the Aircraft Department of Boulton & Paul Aircraft Limited in June 1934. Arising out of delays in production, the Defiant did not enter RAF service until December 1939. The prototype was first flown in 1937. The test pilots identified a number of faults that needed to be rectified, resulting in a second prototype being successfully test-flown in May 1939. The aircraft was designated as the Defiant Mk I.

Powered by a Rolls-Royce Merlin III engine that was rated at 1,030 hp at 16,250 feet, the Defiant's firepower consisted of four belt-fed .303 Browning machine guns in the removable Boulton Paul A Mk IID hydraulically operated dorsal turret. The hydraulic system formed an important part of the turret, which in itself weighed 361lb. Adding 88lb for the four guns, 106lb for the ammunition and 35lb

Airmen from 264 Squadron in front of a Boulton Paul Defiant.

A Defiant on display at RAF Museum Hendon. (Photo Alan Wilson)

for the oxygen equipment and gunsights, the final weight of the loaded Defiant came to 8,318lb, which was 1,657lb more than a Mk I Hawker Hurricane.

The first unit to fly the Defiant was No. 264 Squadron, which operated from RAF Sutton Bridge, and from Marsham Heath from the 1940s. The Defiant made its first appearance, over Dunkirk, during the evacuation of the BEF forces. Initially Luftwaffe fighter pilots mistook the Defiants for Hurricanes, attacking from above and from the rear, which was a grave mistake. The Defiant turret gunners had a field day with the Messerschmitt Bf 109s. But in a very short space of time, however, the turret fighter became known to the Bf 109 pilots and many were shot down by the Luftwaffe who quickly found the aircraft's weaknesses.

No. 141 Squadron, while on its first mission with the Defiant, came into contact with a flight of Bf 109s off the coast at Folkestone. The German fighters shot down two with their first pass, before returning and shooting down four more. No. 264 Squadron suffered a similar fate in August 1940. It had been operationally proven that the Defiant lacked manoeuvrability. It was therefore declared unsuitable for operations on the scale that were taking place during that year and it was withdrawn.

The range of the Defiant was better than that of the Spitfire, but not as good as the Hurricane's. One of the problems was the relatively slow maximum speed. Added to this, it had no forward firing power, and could only rely on the dorsal turret.

At 4:40 a.m. on 4 July 1940, RAF Coltishall, eight miles north of Norwich, saw three Spitfires of No. 66 Squadron fly up to 15,000 feet. Once over Stalham, they came close to a Luftwaffe Dornier Do 17 bomber. A German gunner hit one of the Spitfires forcing it disengage. The other two Spitfires carried on with their attack, finally shooting the Dornier down into the sea. The Battle of Britain had begun.

When the Germans crossed the English Channel, their pilots were tracked by the Observer Corps, with information being relayed by telephone to central observer centres. There were around fifty observer posts for each RAF group area. One such observer centre was located at Norwich.

On 16 July, Hitler issued Directive No. 16: 'As England, in spite of the hopelessness of her military position, has so far shown herself unwilling to come to any compromise, I have decided to begin to prepare for it, and if necessary to carry out, an invasion of England ... if necessary, the island will be occupied.'

With the invasion of Poland on 1 September 1939, all Norwich Corporation work, except for essential services, was suspended. The city council set up an emergency committee, which only had four members at the start: the Lord Mayor, and Aldermen Jex, Riley and Witard.

Hawker Hurricane. (Photo Airwolfhound)

Hawker Typhoons. (Photo RAF)

Vickers Wellington bomber. (Photo RAF)

Spitfire over Norfolk.

Avro Anson. (Photo Bernard Spragg)

Avro Lancaster bomber. (Photo Ronnie Macdonald)

Badges of the Norfolk Regiment

9th Foot, The Norfolk Regt
cap badge
1890s–1937

9th Foot, The Norfolk Regt
shoulder title
1890s–1940s

The Norfolk Regt
cap badge
1937–1958

21st Army Group shoulder flash
Second World War. The 1st Bn
Norfolk Regt was under
command of 3rd Infantry
Division and, in turn, under
command of 21st Army Group.

3rd Infantry Division shoulder
flash Second World War. The
1st Bn Norfolk Regt was under
command of 3rd Infantry
Division in North-West Europe.

2nd Infantry Division shoulder
flash Second World War. The
2nd Bn Norfolk Regt was
under command of 2nd
Infantry Division in Burma.

East Anglian Brigade
cap badge
1958–1969

59th Infantry Division shoulder
flash. Second World War. The 7th
Bn Norfolk Regt was under
command of 59th Infantry Division
in North-West Europe.

Royal Anglian Regt
cap badge
1969 to date

Royal Anglian Regt
regimental arm badge
2000s

1st Bn Royal Anglian Regt
tactical recognition flash
2000s

2nd Bn Royal Anglian Regt
tactical recognition flash
2000s

Royal Anglian Regt
early pattern tactical recognition flash
2000s

© DUDLEY WALL - 2017

IX.TH OR E. NORFOLK REGIMENT OF INFANTRY.

An ENSIGN bearing the REGIMENTAL COLOURS.

& A COLOUR SERJEANT on SERVICE.

9th Regiment of Foot ensign to the colour and NCO.

Early 1800s British soldiers, the 9th Regiment of Foot is on the right.

A sniper with C Company, 2 Royal Anglian, Helmand, Afghanistan.

B-24 Liberator bombers, 93rd Bombardment Group, USAAF, RAF Hardwick.

Tornado GR4, RAF Marham in Norfolk. (Photo MoD)

MILITARY SERVICE ACT, 1916

Every man to whom the Act applies will on Thursday, March 2nd, be deemed to have enlisted for the period of the War unless he is excepted or exempt.

Any man who has adequate grounds for applying to a Local Tribunal for a

CERTIFICATE OF EXEMPTION UNDER THIS ACT

Must do so BEFORE

THURSDAY, MARCH 2

Why wait for the Act to apply to you?

Come now and join of your own free will.

You can at once put your claim for exemption from being called up before a Local Tribunal if you wish.

ATTEST NOW

Published by the PARLIAMENTARY and JOINT LABOUR RECRUITING COMMITTEE, LONDON.   POSTER No. 139   W. K. 1742 10L

Government conscription exemption poster, 1916. (British Government)

Left: The tower is all that remains of St Benedict's Church, bombed in January 1942. (Photo Tanya Dedyukhina)

Below: Norwich Castle. (Photo Qmin)

Right: Boer War Memorial, Norwich. (Photo Tanya Dedyukhina)

Below: Memorial to commemorate the 40th anniversary of the liberation of Helmond, the Netherlands, on 25 September 1944, by the 1st Battalion, Royal Norfolk Regiment. (Photo Edwin J.M. van Lieshout)

Left: The grave of Corporal Sidney Bates VC, 1st Battalion, Royal Norfolk Regiment, Bayeux War Cemetery, Calvados, France. (Photo Ajahewitt)

Below: Guard duty, RAF Marham. In 2008, RAF Marham was granted the Freedom of the City of Norwich. (Photo SAC Andy Masson)

RAF Boeing B-17 Flying Fortress bomber and crew. (Photo RAF)

All branches of the ARP were in full training. Norwich had eleven sirens, and over the next four years, the sirens went off daily, sounding approximately 1,443 times. The Civil Defence had a duty to look after 126,000 people in the city. To cover a worst-case scenario, the authorities formulated plans for the evacuation of Norwich:

Roads to be used to allow evacuation, with a restriction on a two-way flow of civilian traffic: North Walsham Road, Sprowston Road, Bracondale, Ipswich and New Buckenham Roads, Cromer Road, and Earlham Road.

Above: RAF Lancaster bombers, a target's view.

Left: Business end of the Hawker Hurricane fighter.

Above: Handley Page Hampden bombers. (Photo B. J. Daventry, RAF)

Right: Handley Page Halifax heavy bomber.

Gloster Gladiator biplane. (Photo San Diego Air & Space Museum Archives)

Douglas Boston. (Photo San Diego Air & Space Museum Archives)

de Havilland Tiger Moth. (Photo Chris Finney)

de Havilland Mosquito. (Photo Mike Freer)

Bristol Beaufighter.

Bristol Blenheim. (Photo RAF)

One-way military traffic only: Plumstead Road.

Routes for civilian evacuees: into Norwich – Thorpe Road and Salhouse Road, out of Norwich – Newmarket Road and Earlham Green Lane.

Two-way traffic: Drayton Road and Dereham Road.

Civilian refugees on foot, route 1: Thorpe Road, Rose Lane, Cattlemarket Street, Golden Ball Street, All Saints' Green, Grove Road and Grove Walk, Ceil Road, Ipswich Road, Lime Tree Road, and Newmarket Road to County.

Civilian refugees on foot, route 2: Thorpe Road, Carrow Road, King Street, Bracondale Hall Road, Tuckswood Lane, Eaton Road, and Newmarket Road to County.

Connection between the two evacuation routes: Ber Street, Finkelgate and Southwell Road.

Additional refugee routes:

Route 1: Gurney Road, Mousehold Avenue, Lavengro Road, Gertrude Road, Denmark Road, Waterloo Road, Patteson Road, Drayton Road, Waterworks Road, Hotblack Road, Bowthorpe Road, Earlham Green Lane, To County.

Route 2: Catton Grove Road, Philadelphia Road, Stone Road, Drayton Road, Mile Cross Road.

Route 3: Hellesdon Hall Road, Drayton Road, Valpy Avenue, Nelson Street, Alexandra Road, Earlham Road, Christchurch Road, To County

Roads used by the military marked as follows:
Up traffic – black arrow on white background
Down traffic – black arrow on red ground
Two-way traffic – both up and down signs used together

Control-points manned by members of the Military Police:
Boundary Road by Aylsham Road
School Lane by Constitution Hill

Mousehold Lane by Wroxham Road
Plumstead Road by Harvey Lane
Thorpe Road by Harvey Lane
Newmarket Road by Daniels Road
Earlham Road by Colman Road

The air raids started on 3 September 1939 and continued until March 1942. A year before the declaration of war, the people of Norwich had been preparing themselves by building air-raid shelters and placing sandbags around important buildings. At the start of the war, air-raid warnings were sounded, but it would be ten months before Norwich experienced its first attack. Lowestoft would be the first place in East Anglia to suffer loss of life through German bombing.

Most of the raids in 1940 were confined to residential areas, taking place late at night and early in the morning. On 9 July, at around 5 p.m., eleven whistling bombs were dropped by a Dornier Do 17 and a Junkers Ju 88, which landed on and near a warehouse on Salhouse Road. Other bombs fell on Boulton & Paul's at Riverside and Carrow Hill. The company at the time was producing wooden fuselages for Oxford trainer aircraft and nose sections for gliders. It was also here that part of the city wall's Wilderness Tower was destroyed. No air-raid warning had been given and many employees from Colman's were also injured.

Norwich Trades Council called an urgent conference of all unions in the city, before sending a warning to the regional commissioner that production would be greatly disrupted if the warning system was not improved. Within a few days, a statement was made by the clerk of the city: 'I am aware that there is considerable indignation in the city because the air raid sirens are not sounded ... I have spoken personally to the Regional Commissioner, Sir Will Spens, on the telephone and asked him to make urgent representations.'

Ten days later, at 6.15 a.m. bombs damaged or destroyed property at 78 and 80 Bull Close Road, the garage of the Cat & Fiddle Inn, Magdalen Street, 33 and 35 Botolph Street, 172 St George Street and 45 and 47 Pit Street. The Norwich Aero Club rooms, situated just outside the city near Heartsease Lane, were destroyed by fire.

At 6 a.m. on 30 July, a single enemy raider dropped a number of bombs on Victoria Terrace by Pegg's Opening. There had been no warnings, and there were a large number of fatalities when four of a group of five houses collapsed.

Other places bombed were the printing works at Colman's, along with houses in Argyle Street, Compass Street, Ber Street, and the omnibus station on Surrey Street, which was blown to pieces. As a very old historic Norwich building, what remained of the wrecked property was salvaged with a view to restoring the building after the war. However, this too was destroyed by fire in a later raid when the local builder's yard was bombed.

In the afternoon of 1 August, a single enemy raider dropped bombs at the Riverside Works of Boulton & Paul, causing a great blaze in the joinery department and the office. These raids included the first incendiaries to fall within the city boundary. Once again, no warnings had been given, and it was the BBC and the press who reported that Norwich had been hit. This was a first, as newspapers were forbidden from disclosing the name, town or city that had been bombed, except for Dover.

The next day, a meeting took place in London between officials from Norwich City Council and the Ministry of Home Security, urging that sirens should be sounded when an attack on the city was about to take place.

On 10 August, bombs fell on Carrow Works, causing little damage. Ten days later, incendiary bombs were dropped on Surrey Street, Davey Place, the Guildhall and Magdalen Street, where the Home and Colonial Store lost most of its stock.

A bomb fell on Theatre Street on 19 September without exploding. The area was quickly evacuated and it took five days for the disposal squad to defuse the bomb. During the next three months, bombs fell on Orchard Close and Furze Road, where bungalows were destroyed, and on Larkman Lane, Thorpe Hamlet, St John Street, Bracondale, Orchard Tavern, Mountergate and in the Cloister Garth. On 11 December a single bomb hit Dunston Cottages, killing one person.

Shot-down German planes were exhibited in public parks as part of a campaign to increase war savings, called 'Spitfire Funds'. Norwich set the national record by saving £3,386,926.

By the end of September, a news item was released stating that a search had taken place in the gardens of the Bishop's Palace after it was claimed that a bomb could have fallen there. Excavations reached a depth of 30 feet before there was any evidence of a bomb having fallen in the area.

At 6 p.m. on 27 October, a number of high-explosive bombs fell on the outskirts of the city. Bungalows in Orchard Close and Furze Road were also pulled down. On 1 November, Larkman Lane area was hit, but with only slight damage. Thorpe Hamlet was next hit on 11 November.

An Anderson shelter standing relatively intact amid bomb damage in Norwich. (Photo IWM)

The city was attacked again at 6 p.m. on 2 December, which saw houses at 49 St John Street and 49 Bracondale destroyed. The Orchard Tavern at Mountergate was also hit, while a bomb fell in the Cloister Garth of the cathedral, but the only damage was when some modern glass was shattered. During the evening, there were several deaths.

The demolition of Dunston Cottages, just by Carrow Hill, took place after a bombing raid on 11 December. The last raids of the year took place on the evening of 21 December, when a high-explosive bomb was dropped in Rye Avenue, Mile Cross. A number of residential properties were damaged, but no casualties were reported.

Although fewer bombs fell in 1941 compared to the previous year, damage to property was greater, and there were twenty-one fatalities. In the late morning of 5 January, a number of bombs were dropped on Eaton Golf Club and the City of Norwich School playing fields. Unthank Road found itself being machine-gunned, resulting only in smashed windows and tiles.

Boulton & Paul's Riverside Works was hit once again on 4 February. Vauxhall Street, in the early hours of the morning on 18 February, was bombed, in which numerous houses and business premises were destroyed. Eight people were killed and a large number injured. Salhouse Road was bombed again on 27 February – this time Barnard's Factory was hit.

On 14 March, up to forty incendiary bombs dropped in St Benedict's Street, luckily causing little damage. Other bombs doing little damage were dropped on 30 March on Caernarvon Road, and the house of the sheriff Mr W. J. Finch at 130 Earlham Road. There were few injuries, although one occupant had to be rescued from the wreckage.

A drayman from Steward & Patteson was killed on 2 April when bombs were dropped in Riverside. Houses and businesses were also machine-gunned. While the Quarter Sessions were sitting at the Shirehall, a bomb came through the roof without hurting anyone. Colman's was targeted on 29 April, with several mills set on fire. Unthank Road was once again hit on 5 May, along with Bury Street. In the city, a bomb was dropped on the roof of St Michael at Plea, and although there were many casualties, including three fatalities, the fire was put out very quickly.

On 7 May, many houses were hit and destroyed on the Larkman Lane Estate, resulting in the death of Mr and Mrs Britcher and three of their six children. Three days later, numerous bombs were dropped in Cecil Road near the APR post. On 17 May, heavy bombs were dropped at Old Lakenham and in Martineau Lane. The 30 July raid saw stick bombs dropped in Marl Pit Lane and Dereham Road, but causing little structural damage.

During the late afternoon on 10 May, five bombs were dropped in Cecil Road. A direct hit on a flat in Lady Betty Road completely destroyed the property. Grove Walk was also hit, including a house at the rear that belonged to Mr Clifford White, the 1941/2 Sherriff. In the early hours of 17 May, two heavy bombs dropped on Old Lakenham, causing damage to many properties.

In the small hours of the morning of 30 July, stick bombs were dropped near Marl Pit Lane and in Dereham Road, but without much damage being caused. The last of the heavy bombing on Norwich took place on 8 August. A bomb that fell near Church Farm, Eaton, failed to explode.

The Baedeker Blitz, or Baedeker raids, were raids conducted by the Luftwaffe on British cities in direct response to the RAF's increasingly destructive bombing of Nazi Germany, which started with the raid on Lübeck in March 1942. The name is derived from a German Foreign Office statement at the time that declared that all English cities listed with 3 stars in the travel book, *Baedeker Guide,* would be bombed into oblivion.

The first Baedeker Raids took place on 27 April, lasting for well over four hours. The sirens sounded and a vicious night raid took place. Two pathfinder aircraft released their flares then incendiary bombs. Norwich railway station was attacked first, before a further twenty-six aircraft arrived in waves of threes and fours to unleash their ordnance. This continued unopposed for over ten minutes before the RAF fighters arrived.

The assault lasted for over an hour. Around fifty tons of bombs – over 185 heavy bombs – were dropped over the city in 103 separate incidents. Among the buildings hit were the Norwich Social Welfare Institution, the Norwich Institute for the Blind, the Regal Cinema, the Hippodrome, Mand Department Stores, Curl's, Woolworth's, Boots, Bunting's, Bowhill & Hubbard, Edwards & Holmes, Coleman's Wincarnis Works, Norwich Union and many others, but many old historical buildings escaped major damage.

Schools, places of worship and public houses were hit. The many casualties included firewatchers, ambulance men and men of the Home Guard. The area most hit was Heigham Street, where the majority of buildings were reduced

Norwich City Station, 1900s.

to rubble. St Augustine's School was all but destroyed, and the roof of the Odeon Cinema in Boltolph Street damaged. Part of the Grapes Hotel was gutted.

A few weeks before the raids, the city staged a firefighting exercise over a two-night period, working on the presumption that there were up to fifty fires blazing simultaneously, involving the many shoe factories, public houses and places of worship. In all, over 1,000 firefighters took part.

On 29 and 30 April, Norwich sought protection in Anderson, Morrison and street shelters. The raiders came with the same pattern that lasted for

Norfolk & Norwich Hospital, June 1942

seventy-five minutes. Rampant Horse Street was hit, and Curl's department store badly damaged. The Boar's Head Inn, Caley's, Clarke's Shoe Factory, Baker Engineering Factory and St Mary's Silk Mills all took hits. This turned out to be another heavy attack, with over forty-five tons of bombs – 112 heavy bombs – being dropped. The new RAF Mosquito fighter went into action, but they were not able to stop the raiders. There were many deaths, and burials took place at the Norwich Cemetery on 4, 5 and 7 May.

On 1 May, just after one in the morning, enemy aircraft scattered 700 incendiaries over Heigham Street, Duke Street and St Andrew's Street. Strong winds fanned the flames, but it was the quick-thinking wardens and fireguards moving into action that ameliorated the situation

In defiance, most of the stores that had been bombed started to trade again, albeit from different buildings. By the time the next raids took place, just after midnight on 9 May, strengthened defences had been put into place. RAF fighters performed thirty-seven sorties. New anti-aircraft guns were in action for the full thirty-minute assault.

Norfolk & Norwich Hospital visit by King George VI, October 1942.

On 26 May, the Duke of Kent visited the city to boost morale. In front of City Hall, he met the Civil Defence services and members of the Home Guard.

On 27 June 1942, wards at the Norfolk & Norwich Hospital were hit, along with the main operating theatre and the nurses' home. The Thatched Assembly Rooms was also hit. An incredible 850 incendiaries were dropped on the cathedral, but owing to the firewatchers and the fact that the Cathedral is built of stone and brick, little damage was done, although a house in the Close was gutted. St Michael at Thorn Church, situated in Ber Street, and St Paul's were both burned out. There was virtually nothing left of St Julian's Church in King Street and the synagogue in Synagogue Street, a street that no longer exists. RAF night-fighters could be heard above the noise of the Luftwaffe aircraft, as fires spread over the rooftops of the city with a deafening noise.

On 28 July, high-explosive bombs were dropped over St Benedict's Church. Brett's suffered when the two top storeys were burned out. The sleeping quarters at nearby Bullard's was destroyed.

There were more attacks on 2 August when furniture-makers Trevor Page of St John Maddermarket was hit, along with Beck's wine shop in Exchange Street and Frost's tool shop in Lobster Lane. The shoe factory of Sexton Sons & Everard that formed part of St Mary's Plain was gutted. Hurrell's, the shoe factory situated at 100 Magdalen Street, was also burned out. Widespread fires were started by a flux of incendiaries.

By the end of 1942, Norwich had been through 106 bombing alerts over a period of 99 hours, leaving over 30,000 dwellings damaged and over 2,000 destroyed. When the raids took place Norwich's Civil Defence was joined by teams from all over East Anglia, including the RAF.

On 5 September, bombs were dropped on Magdalen Street, killing five and injuring many others. On 19 October, bombs were dropped in Carrow, and by late morning, the Jenny Lind Children's Playground in Pottergate lay in ruins. November and December saw bombs fall in Cattlemarket, All Saints Green and the bus station on Surrey Street. Morgan's brewery in King Street was badly damaged, but the offices situated in their seventeenth-century Howard House were almost unscathed. Ground targets were also machine-gunned. The last attack of the year took place on 5 December at 1 p.m, when bombs were dropped near the Heartsease Inn, but with no damage.

The city instituted its own Air Training Corps, followed by the Sea Cadet Corps, a trend that soon took place throughout the eastern counties. Members of the

Norwich division of the Air Training Corps, aged between 16 and 18, were trained to gain experience of what life was like in the RAF.

In 1942, the Warship Weeks commenced throughout the country, at which bands played and models of warships and machines were exhibited for all to see. Norwich announced that it would be raising £1 million for the cost of a cruiser that would be named HMS *Norfolk*. Sir Kinsley Wood, Chancellor of the Exchequer, came to the city to discuss this. He suggested that the city should be able to raise more and the final total raised was £1,392,649.

Norwich burns.

The law courts remained just as busy during wartime. Two young men, privates of the Royal Norfolk Regiment, were sentenced to six months at Norwich for breaking into a house. Three others were sent to Borstal for a period of three years after getting caught trying to break into a shop after going absent without leave. One soldier, who had come to Norwich to help out the National Fire Service (NFS) during the raids, entered a bombed office where he stole items valued at £2/2. He was sentenced to three months in prison.

On New Year's Day, 1943, bombs were dropped near North Heigham, but there were no casualties. In another attack, a bomb hit the south wall of St Barnabas Church, damaging the roof and some of the stained-glass windows.

The next bombs were dropped on 18 March. The clothing factory of F. W. Harmer in St Andrew's Street was hit and burned to the ground. Three people were injured and taken to hospital. Similar attacks took place with residential properties being hit

In the early hours of 5 May, bombs were dropped around the St Andrew's area. A bakery in Bridewell Alley and nearby premises in Queen Street, the Cathedral Restaurant and Estate Agent Bells were destroyed, while Plowright's Antique Dealers suffered damage. The tower of St Andrew's Parish Church was also hit. Bombs just outside the city hit the areas of Larkman Lane and Hellesdon, but because of alert firewatchers and the efficient NFS, damage was very limited.

Norwich railway station was bombed on 7 October, but only slight damage was sustained. On 6 November, just after midnight, bombs were dropped in the Unthank Road area, causing two fires that were quickly bought under control. This was to be the last time that Norwich was bombed.

During the last two years of the war, no further bombs fell on Norwich. September and October 1944 saw German V2 rockets dropping in Norfolk, but the closest any came to Norwich was when one came down on the Royal Norwich Golf Course at Hellesdon.

On the afternoon of 24 November, an American aircraft was flying over Norwich when its wing tip hit the tower of St Philip's Church on Heigham Road. This resulted in structural damage to the building and the aircraft crashing. In an act of bravery, the pilot steered the plane so that it did not hit a row of houses in Heigham Street, crashing instead on grounds near the railway. The crew were all killed. A plaque remembering their gallantry was placed on a house nearby, which was unveiled in November 1945 by General E. C. Kiel, commanding officer of the 8th Fighter Command, US Air Force.

During the Blitz, Norwich suffered numerous casualties, particularly in 1942:

Year	Killed	Injured	Total
1940	60	190	240
1941	21	104	125
1942	258	784	1,042
1943	1	14	15

At the outbreak of the war in 1939, Norwich had 35,569 houses, a statistic that puts into perspective the damage to residential properties caused by the Blitz:

Destroyed	2,082
Seriously damaged	2,651
Moderately damaged	25,621
Total	30,354

During 1944, Norwich saw very few enemy aircraft, but on the evening of 22 April, several American B-24 Liberator bombers were shot down while on their way back from daylight operations. The crews had not been trained in night flying, so they experienced difficulties in landing their aircraft without being sitting ducks for the enemy. One of the B-24s that was shot down, crashed just outside Norwich in Tuckswood.

That year, the USAAF 467th Bombardment Group from Rackheath, known as the 'Rackheath Aggies', flew a total of 212 missions and a total of 5,538 sorties. The USAAF 458th Bombardment Group, who were stationed at Horsham St Faiths, flew 240 missions with 5,759 sorties.

The 1st Battalion Royal Norfolk Regiment was in India when the war broke out. They came back to England in 1940 to be given home defence duties, and later participated in the D-Day invasion in June 1944. The 2nd and 7th battalions were in France at the start of the war, serving with the British Expeditionary Force. The 2nd Battalion saw action in Burma, while the 4th, 5th and 6th battalions served in the Far East theatre. By 1943, there were seventeen Norfolk Home Guard battalions.

In 2012, a house in Norwich, called Pinebanks, was discovered to have been an underground wireless station that had been set up in 1940 in order to monitor the planned German invasion. Churchill had set up a secret force, called GHQ Auxiliary

American soldiers in Norwich enjoying fish and chips.

Units, with certain branches acquiring the status of 'special duties'. These units were mainly used in the south-east and East Anglia to spy and report on German military activities. The station was manned by civilians, who would send and receive messages for the military. It had a fake bookshelf that concealed an entrance to the radio room and an escape tunnel. Described as a rare find by British historians, Pinebanks Station at Thorpe St Andrews was given heritage protection in 2016.

Over 15,000 East Anglian men served in the 18th Infantry Division, a second-line duplicate of the 54th (East Anglian) Infantry Division. The 4th, 5th, 6th and

7th battalions of the Royal Norfolk Regiment were transferred to the new division, as part of the 53rd Infantry Brigade.

The 4th Battalion was originally based at Chapelfield Drill Hall, under Commanding Officer Lieutenant Colonel J. H. Jewson. The battalion then moved to Great Yarmouth for intensive training, and, in 1941, to Hardwick in Scotland. The soldiers were uncertain as to where their overseas posting would be. In October 1941, second-in-command Lieutenant Colonel A. E. Knights MC, MM took over from Jewson who had been promoted. After news was received that the Japanese had attacked Pearl Harbour on 9 December 1941, and that Britain and America were now at war with Japan, the 4th sailed to Mombasa, where they spent Christmas Day on the Indian Ocean. Days later, they arrived at Ahmednagar in India, and at the end of the month, they disembarked at Keppel Harbour in Singapore.

In the words of a Norwich soldier who was there:

The convoy sailed from Bombay at 13.00 hours on the 19 January, its destination being given as the south west Pacific Area. Pamphlets on jungle warfare were issued, and all ranks attempted to learn something of the new type of warfare which lay ahead. As the convoy passed through the Banker Straits on 28 January, it was sighted by a Japanese plane which dropped six bombs without result. That night, in order to avoid any bunching of the ships in narrow waters, the three fastest vessels were ordered ahead at full speed. The USS *Wakefield* won the race to Singapore and 54 Brigade disembarked in Keppel Harbour, Singapore, on the 2nd. Although the news from Malaya was not encouraging, spirits were high in the battalion [4th Royal Norfolks]. It could not yet be known that, within a period of seventeen days, all the months of training since 1939 were to be wasted. The curtain was only just beginning to rise on the last act of the great tragedy.

Such was my introduction to Singapore and 3¼ years as a P.O.W. of the Japanese. Within two days of our arrival the Causeway across Johore Straits was blown and Singapore Island, separated from the main land, was hurriedly prepared for a last stand against the enemy.

The 4th Royal Norfolk, in which Battalion I was a company commander, went abroad 950 strong. In five days fighting, 10 officers and 147 other ranks were killed, and 8 officers and 115 other ranks wounded.

Similar casualties were suffered by all the other East Anglian regiments, namely the 5th and 6th Royal Norfolks, 4th and 5th Suffolks, 1st and 2nd Cambridgeshires, with their brigade and divisional troops.

The 'Railway of Death' was built at a cost of 13,000 British, Australian and Dutch lives, and thousands more of coolies from Malaya. That, however, ignores completely the many thousands of prisoners who died as a result of the hardships in captivity, or whose lives were forever affected by all they had endured and suffered.

Three years and nine months after the fall of Singapore, there was a Sunday service held in St Peter Mancroft in the centre of Norwich on 4 November 1945, for thanksgiving and remembrance on behalf of the returned prisoners of war and their families. As was reported in the *Eastern Daily Press* the next day, long before the service commenced with the singing of the national anthem, every pew and every available chair was occupied. The service was conducted by Canon C. C. Lanchester in a church that was still lit by gaslight and with the great East Window boarded up against the elements. The paper reported: 'Finally the Bishop asked all to remember that their duty was to look forward and not back. God had served them from a terrible fate with a purpose. That purpose was to play their part in building a new life in which war and its evils would no longer be possible.'

For the heroes of Norwich, the fall of Singapore heralded a time of unimaginable hardship, deprivation, brutality and horror that no amount of reading can comprehend. Yet, as always, the human spirit managed to evince gentleness with those whose will could not withstand the onslaught of enslavement. All this and more was in the minds of those who had gathered to honour fallen comrades, and to renew contacts with living ones. It was said, by people at the service, that they were humbled and amazed that such things could have been endured by men who look like everyone's bank manager, office worker, electrician, postman, father, uncle and grandfather.

It was a splendid service, a soldier's service – sincere, direct, moving and totally unsentimental. It seemed so right that the plaque in St Peter Mancroft offers succour to the families of those who died so far from home and for whom there is no other memorial, save in their children and grandchildren.

Norfolk's beaches, including Thornham, were constantly practise-bombed by the Allies in the build-up to D-Day, so as to test the impact of their efforts. After being analyzed by geologists who were assisting military planners, the beach at Brancaster was considered to be the nearest match to the Normandy coast.

The 1st Battalion, Royal Norfolk Regiment, having been recalled from India during the Battle of Britain, went on to fight with distinction during the Normandy – landing on Sword Beach at 0725 hours on 6 June 1944 – and North West Europe campaigns. Of all the battalions in his 21st Army Group, Field Marshal Sir Bernard Montgomery claimed that the 1st Battalion was 'second to none'. From June 1944 until the end of the war, the 1st Battalion suffered 20 officers and 260 other ranks killed and over 1,000 wounded or missing, over 1,300 casualties in all. Of the ORs killed was Corporal Sidney Bates who was posthumously awarded the Victoria Cross for his heroism during the fight at Sourdeval on 8 August 1944 (see his citation in the following chapter).

The 2nd Battalion, Royal Norfolk Regiment was involved in covering the 1940 retreat to Dunkirk, valiantly and against all odds holding the line of the La Bassée Canal. Elements of the HQ Company were involved in a stubborn defence of a farmhouse before being overwhelmed. Ninety-nine soldiers surrendered to a unit of the SS Totenkopf (Death's Head) Division before being lined up against a barn wall and machine-gunned. Privates Pooley and O'Callaghan managed to survive the massacre by hiding in a pigsty. The bodies of the murdered troops were exhumed in 1942 by the French and reburied in the local churchyard which now forms part of the Le Paradis War Cemetery. Knoechlein, the SS commander, was brought to justice and hanged in 1949 in Hamburg. A memorial plaque was placed on the barn wall in 1970. On a happier note, the 2nd Battalion, later in the war and still under the auspices of the 4th Infantry Brigade, 2nd Infantry Division of the Fourteenth Army, served in the Burma Campaign at the Battle of Kohima, one of many such battles it fought in the Far East theatre under Field Marshal Bill Slim, arguably Britain's finest general of the war.

Five members of the Royal Norfolks, the highest number of any British regiment during the Second World War, were awarded the Victoria Cross: David Auldjo Jamieson, John Niel Randle, George Gristock, Sidney Bates and George Arthur Knowland (Randle and Knowland posthumously for extraordinary heroism in the Far East). Their citations appear in the following chapter.

Post 1945

After Japan surrendered in 1945, the 2nd Battalion found itself on duty in India, where they saw service in Calcutta and Rawalpindi. They had to deal with much unrest and violence, the fallout of Partition. The battalion remained until independence on 17 August 1947. They left on HMT *Georgic*, the first troopship to leave India.

Just after the war ended, Korea, formally a Japanese colony, was split into two. The north became known as the Democratic People's Republic of Korea, which fell under Soviet administration, while the south became the Republic of Korea, under American administration. In June 1950, North Korea crossed the border between north and south, the 38th Parallel, causing the outbreak of war, which lasted for three years. The United Nations, with largely American forces, came to the assistance of South Korea. The 1st Battalion, Royal Norfolk Regiment, arrived in Korea November 1951 and stayed for ten months, mainly in the front line. As well as helping to dig a trench system, laying ambushes and sending out patrols, the battalion was awarded many awards for gallantry, but also saw over 33 killed with 108 injured. Reflecting general sentiment, a soldier later stated: 'Nobody told us what the war was about. We just picked it up as we went along. To be honest, when we were out there we did not know if we were fighting for the North or South; it was as bad as that, because it had all been put on us and within two weeks we were on the move. We used to think why are we put here, what's it all about.'

UN forces retreat south over the border, the 38th Parallel.

In 1951, 18-year-old commercial artist from Norwich, Ray Segon, was told to report to Britannia Barracks. He remembers parading in civilian clothes, and being told in an address by an officer that they were joining the finest regiment in the British Army, and that they would be joining the 1st Battalion in Korea. Segon was also informed that those who did their training well would come back and those who didn't would not.

The 1st Battalion was then moved from Korea to Hong Kong and the nearby New Territories in September 1952, for a two-year tour of duty. During this period, the battalion helped in training locals in case of a Chinese invasion. In November 1955, the 1st Battalion was sent to Cyprus as part of a 25,000-man British peacekeeping force (mainly curfew control and roadblock duties) on the island and former colony, in an effort to suppress Georgios Grivas's anti-British terrorist organization EOKA (National Organization of Cypriot Fighters) that had the benign blessing of the Greek Cypriot leader Archbishop Makarios. The battalion was withdrawn in 1959 with the implementation of a peace treaty.

'Old Contemptibles' of the 1914 British Expeditionary Force (BEF) gather at City Hall Norwich, 1950.

4. THEY SERVED

Armiger Watts Hubbard

The headstone to Armiger Watts Hubbard (1783–1844) that once stood in St Augustine's churchyard in Norwich no longer exists, having been lost when part of the churchyard was converted into a public garden by the Norwich Corporation in 1894. The inscription on the headstone, however, had been transcribed for posterity in the 1870s:

> To the Memory of
> ARMIGER WATTS HUBBARD
> Lieut. in the Royal Marines
> who serv'd on board the Royal Sovereign
> the Flag Ship of
> Admiral Lord Collingwood
> at the celebrated battle of Trafalgar
> He died Febry. 14th 1844
> Aged 60 Years.

Hubbard, whose unusual first name translates as 'bearing arms', enlisted in the Royal Marines at the age of 15. By the age of 22, he was transferred from Royal Marine Company No. 44, Portsmouth, to the 100-gun ship HMS *Royal Sovereign*, the flagship of Vice-Admiral Cuthbert Collingwood, who was Nelson's second-in-command and oldest of friends.

During the Battle of Trafalgar, Lieutenant Hubbard escaped without serious injury. A day after the battle and following the death of Nelson, Admiral Collingwood wrote: 'Where can I find language to express my sentiments of the valour and skill which were displayed by the Officers, the Seamen and Marines in the battle with the enemy, where every individual appeared a hero on whom the glory of his country depended?' For his part in the battle, Hubbard was awarded by Parliament the sum of £108 12s 0d, with an additional prize money of £44 4s 6d. By the age of 58, Hubbard was a resident at a girl's boarding school in St George's Plain, living with his daughter-in-law, Mary Ann Wright Hubbard, who was the school's governess. Hubbard died after a short illness on Valentine's

Day 1884, ten days before his 61st birthday. It is not known why he was buried in St Augustine's Churchyard.

Sir Edward Berry

Berry was born 1768, the son of a London merchant who had died at an early age, leaving a widow with seven children and very little money. Berry was educated by his uncle in Norwich, before, with the help of a patronage through Lord Mulgrave, joining the navy as a midshipman on HMS *Burford*. He went on to become a signal midshipman on HMS *Duke*. While attacking the French man-of-war *St Pierre* in Martinique, Berry was standing on the poop deck when a shot passed near him, causing him to collapse. Thinking he was dead, he was taken below where he shocked everyone by gaining a full recovery. Promoted to lieutenant for bravery, he came to the attention of Admiral Sir John Jervis via a letter written to him by Nelson. Berry would later be appointed first lieutenant to Nelson on HMS *Agamemnon*. Knighted and given the rank of rear admiral, Berry died in 1831.

George Wilde

George Wilde, 13th Light Dragoons, was born in the parish of St Margaret's, Norwich. He enlisted at Norwich on 27 August 1842, aged 18 years and 5 months. Records trace the rest of his life:

> He went from being private to corporal, and on 16 December 1855 he trans-
> ferred to the 4th Bn. of the Military Train, as Cpl. vide War Office Authority,
> dated the 14 of October, on the 1 of November 1856. Regtl. No. 1002'. He resigned
> to Pte. on the 1 of July 1857. He was discharged from the Royal Victoria Hospital,
> Netley, on the 26 of February 1867 ... He was found unfit for further service. Has
> Chronic Rheumatism. Disease did not exist before enlistment and is therefore
> the result of long service and exposure – had broken-down constitution which
> will materially affect his ability to earn his livelihood. He had served 24 years
> 157 days in Turkey, 2 years in the Crimea and 2 years 2 months in New Zealand.
> His conduct was exemplary and he was in possession of four G C badges. Once
> entered in the Regimental Defaulter's Book but never tried by Court-martial.

Wilde was entitled to the Crimean and Turkish medals. The census of 1881 shows him living at Gladstone Street, Heigham, a 'Private Chelsea Pensioner'. He died on 18 May 1887. An extract from the *Norfolk Annals* for 12 May 1887 states: 'Died at Gladstone Street, Norwich, George Wilde, aged 62, the last survivor in the City of the famous light cavalry brigade charge at Balaclava. Wilde was then present with the 13th Light Dragoons, his horse being killed under him and he himself being wounded. He was in receipt of a pension of 13d per day.' Wilde is buried in the Rosary Cemetery in Grave No 1a/125.

Sergeant Henry Cator VC

Henry Cator (24 January 1894–7 April 1966) was a recipient of the Victoria Cross, the highest award for gallantry that can be awarded to a member of British and Commonwealth forces. Born in Drayton, Cator joined the army in September 1914, and arrived on the Western Front in June 1915. As a sergeant at Hangest Trench, Arras on 4 October 1917, he brought back thirty-six wounded men from no man's land under heavy fire. His citation reads:

> For most conspicuous bravery and devotion to duty. Whilst consolidating the first line captured system his platoon suffered severe casualties from hostile machine-gun and rifle fire. In full view of the enemy and under heavy fire Sergeant Cator, with one man, advanced to cross the open to attack the hostile machine gun. The man accompanying him was killed after going a short distance, but Sergeant Cator continued on and picking up a Lewis gun and some drums on his way succeeded in reaching the northern end of the hostile trench. Meanwhile, one of our bombing parties was seen to be held up by a machine gun. Sergeant Cator took up a position from which he sighted this gun and killed the entire team and the officer whose papers he brought in. He continued to hold that end of the trench with the Lewis gun and with such effect that the bombing squad was enabled to work along, the result being that one hundred prisoners and five machine guns were captured.

Days later, Henry was caught in an exploding shell. He was also awarded the French Croix de Guerre. After the war, he was employed as a postman, and during the Second World War he served as a captain in the Home Guard. He died in Norwich and is buried in Sprowston Cemetery. His medals were sold in 1985 for £10,500.

Henry Montgomery Scott-Pillow

Scott-Pillow was born on 31 March 1895 to Mrs Margaret Eleanor Pillow of 10a Castle Meadow, Norwich. After school, he went on in 1914 to study as a dental student at

Guy's Hospital. He then joined the Public Schools Corps and was soon given a commission in the Middlesex Regiment. He went to France in 1917, where he was killed in action on 8 August while attached to the 7th Squadron, Royal Flying Corps. His commanding officer wrote these words to his mother: 'Your son has shown himself a very promising and capable pilot who always did his work well, and he endeared himself to all whom he came in contact.' In reports, Henry's surname varies between Pillow and Scott-Pillow. His birth certificate shows him as Henry Montague S. Pillow and in the register at Guy's it is shown as 'Pillow, Henry Montague Scott'. On a Guy's list of serving men in October 1916, he is shown as 'Pillow, H. M. S'. On the Church of St Peter Mancroft War Memorial, his name appears as 'Pillow, Henry'. There are records held at the Norfolk Record office that show him as 'Henry Montague Pillow', while his membership certificate to the Carlyle Club, 211 Piccadilly, dated 3 November 1916, gives his name as Henry M. S. Pillow.

Hezekiah Edward Youngs

Born in Norwich on 29 August 1891 to Hezekiah and Elvera Youngs, Youngs's life is commemorated on page 355 of the *First World War Book of Remembrance.*

Private Hezekiah Youngs and (*facing*) his attestation form, 1916.

ATTESTATION PAPER.

No. 679215

Folio.

CANADIAN OVER-SEAS EXPEDITIONARY FORCE.

QUESTIONS TO BE PUT BEFORE ATTESTATION.

(ANSWERS.)

1. What is your surname?	Youngs
1a. What are your Christian names?	Hezekiah Edward
1b. What is your present address?	113 Bathurst St
2. In what Town, Township or Parish, and in what Country were you born?	Norwich Norfolk Eng
3. What is the name of your next-of-kin?	Hezekiah Edward Youngs
4. What is the address of your next-of-kin?	137 Essex St Norwich Eng
4a. What is the relationship of your next-of-kin?	father
5. What is the date of your birth?	Aug 29th 1891
6. What is your Trade or Calling?	laborer
7. Are you married?	no
8. Are you willing to be vaccinated or re-vaccinated and inoculated?	yes
9. Do you now belong to the Active Militia?	no
10. Have you ever served in any Military Force? If so, state particulars of former Service.	no
11. Do you understand the nature and terms of your engagement?	yes
12. Are you willing to be attested to serve in the CANADIAN OVER-SEAS EXPEDITIONARY FORCE?	yes

DECLARATION TO BE MADE BY MAN ON ATTESTATION.

I, Hezekiah Edward Youngs, do solemnly declare that the above are answers made by me to the above questions and that they are true, and that I am willing to fulfil the engagements by me now made, and I hereby engage and agree to serve in the Canadian Over-Seas Expeditionary Force, and to be attached to any arm of the service therein, for the term of one year, or during the war now existing between Great Britain and Germany should that war last longer than one year, and for six months after the termination of that war provided His Majesty should so long require my services, or until legally discharged.

Hezekiah Edward Youngs (Signature of Recruit)

(Signature of Witness)

Date Jan 31 191 6

OATH TO BE TAKEN BY MAN ON ATTESTATION.

I, Hezekiah Edward Youngs, do make Oath, that I will be faithful and bear true Allegiance to His Majesty King George the Fifth, His Heirs and Successors, and that I will as in duty bound honestly and faithfully defend His Majesty, His Heirs and Successors, in Person, Crown and Dignity, against all enemies, and will observe and obey all orders of His Majesty, His Heirs and Successors, and of all the Generals and Officers set over me. So help me God.

Hezekiah Edward Youngs (Signature of Recruit)

(Signature of Witness)

Date Jan 31 191 6

CERTIFICATE OF MAGISTRATE.

The Recruit above-named was cautioned by me that if he made any false answer to any of the above questions he would be liable to be punished as provided in the Army Act.

The above questions were then read to the Recruit in my presence.

I have taken care that he understands each question, and that his answer to each question has been duly entered as replied to, and the said Recruit has made and signed the declaration and taken the oath

before me, at Toronto this 31 day of Jan 191 6

(Signature of Justice)

M. F. W. 23.
200 M.—11-15.
H. Q. 1772-39-811.

Lieut Col.

He died on 16 July 1917 and is buried at Aix-Noulette Communal Cemetery Extension, Pas de Calais, France, with grave reference number I. G. 10. Hezekiah and his family lived in a Victorian terraced house at 137 Essex Street, which today does not exist and is probably now part of the Jenny Lind Playground. At a young age, Hezekiah moved to Canada, and by 1916 he was serving with the 20th Battalion, the Canadian Infantry.

John and Thomas Howard

John Howard was born in the mid-1420s to Sir Robert Howard of Stoke-by-Nayland, Suffolk, and Margaret, coheiress of Thomas Mowbray. John Howard was knighted in 1461 and held many military titles under Edward IV. He became a strong supporter of Richard III and was created First Duke of Norfolk in June 1483. After the king's death at Bosworth, Howard commanded Richard's army.

Thomas Howard, Earl of Surrey, and later second Duke of Norfolk, was born in 1443. During the Battle of Bosworth, he was injured and taken prisoner. During the first Parliament of Henry VII, he was stripped of all his titles and spent three years as a prisoner in the Tower of London. In 1514, his titles were restored by Henry VIII. The Howards played a prominent role in the military legacy of Norwich.

Corporal Sidney James Day VC

His citation for the award of the Victoria Cross appeared in *The London Gazette* on 17 October 1917:

Corporal Sidney James Day.

No. 15092 Cpl. Sidney James Day, Suff. R. (Norwich).

For most conspicuous bravery.

Cpl. Day was in command of a bombing section detailed to clear a maze of trenches still held by the enemy; this he did, killing two machine gunners and taking four prisoners. On reaching a point where the trench had been levelled, he went alone and bombed his way through to the left, in order to gain touch with the neighbouring troops. Immediately on his return to his section a stick bomb fell into a trench occupied by two officers (one badly wounded) and three other ranks. Cpl. Day seized the bomb and threw it over the trench, where it immediately exploded. This prompt action undoubtedly saved the lives of those in the trench. He afterwards completed the clearing of the trench, and, establishing himself in an advanced position, remained for sixty-six hours at his post, which came under intense hostile shell and rifle grenade fire. Throughout the whole operations his conduct was an inspiration to all.

Flight Lieutenant Steve Stevens DFC and Maud Stevens (née Miller)

Steve Stevens, a Second World War bomber, met his wife Maud Miller when, as a telephone operator, she helped to guide him back to safety at RAF Scampton in Lincolnshire from a bombing mission over Germany. Maud was a member of the Women's Auxiliary Air Force (WAAF) which saw her play a vital role in the Dambusters Raid, talking the returning crews back to land after the mission during the early hours of 17 May 1943.

The strike had been led by Commander Guy Gibson, in which aircraft of No. 617 Squadron employed bouncing bombs to shatter the Moehne and Eder dams, sending floodwaters pouring into the Ruhr Valley. It was not long afterwards that the 21-year-old pilot, who would be awarded the Distinguished Flying Cross (DFC), asked Miss Miller out on a date. Eight months later they were married in Maud's home city, Norwich.

The majority of Stevens's missions were over Germany. However, he also conducted three sorties over Italy, including a 2,200-mile flight to Turin. This would be the longest distance for a raid carried out by Bomber Command. Just before his wedding in November 1943, Flight Lieutenant Stevens shook hands with George VI, after being awarded the DFC.

Sir Thomas Erpingham

Sir Thomas Erpingham KG (c.1355–1428), was an English knight who became famous as the commander of King Henry V's longbow-wielding archers at the Battle of Agincourt. He was immortalized as a character in the play *Henry V* by William Shakespeare. It is, however, his lengthy and loyal service to John of Gaunt, Henry IV and Henry V, which contributed significantly to the establishment of the House of Lancaster on the English throne. This is his true legacy.

In April 1415, Erpingham indentured to serve with a company of eighty men on King Henry's forthcoming expedition to France. The eighty included twenty men-at-arms and sixty archers. When the company mustered in Southampton, it consisted of twenty-four men-at-arms and seventy-three archers. The army crossed to France in August, where Erpingham's men were involved in the Siege of Harfleur. After Harfleur, the remaining men of Erpingham's company marched with the king towards Calais. On 25 October, the English fought the French army at Agincourt. Erpingham was stationed in the main battle, alongside King Henry. Despite his long military career, it was his first major battle. As an experienced soldier, however, Henry gave him the task of marshalling his archers. He is recorded as having ridden across the front of the army to carry out his duties. When he was satisfied that the archers were in position, he threw his marshal's baton into the air and shouted what French listeners heard as '*Nestroque*'. This has commonly been interpreted as a rendition of 'now strike'. Erpingham then dismounted and joined the king. After the battle, Erpingham marched with the army to Calais, where he embarked with the king in November to return to England.

Erpingham was a significant benefactor to the city of Norwich, where, in 1420, he had built the cathedral gate which bears his name, opposite the west door of the Norwich Cathedral leading into Cathedral Close. A kneeling statue of Erpingham is found in a niche in the centre of the tall, flint-faced gable of the Erpingham Gate. He is buried on the north side of the presbytery of the cathedral.

Major General Sir Vincent Eyre KCSI, CB

When the Franco-Prussian War broke out in August 1870, Major General Sir Vincent Eyre, a retired 59-year-old, was in France. This was the first war to take place in north-west Europe since the Battle of Waterloo half a century earlier. Much had changed since then, such as Florence Nightingale's revolutionary changes to nursing, and the Geneva Convention of 1864, which provided for the medical personnel of the armed forces and the Red Cross Society. Major General Sir Vincent and Lady Eyre, as part of the English Red Cross Society, had already formed a committee in Boulogne to raise a British volunteer ambulance service that provided medical staff and vehicles to collect and treat the wounded on the battlefields across northern France. Military officers became involved, along with the nurses trained by Florence Nightingale.

Eyre was born in 1811, just four years before the Battle of Waterloo. Educated at Norwich Grammar School, he entered the Military Academy at Addiscombe. In 1828, he was gazetted to the Bengal establishment, arriving in Calcutta on 21 May 1829. Within eight years, he was promoted to first lieutenant in the Horse Artillery Company. In 1842, in the First Afghan War, while in command of two guns at Kabul, he was severely wounded and captured along with his family. Eyre was one of only a dozen or so to survive out of approximately

MAJOR VINCENT EYRE.

Vincent Eyre.

4,500 soldiers and some 12,000 civilians during the infamous Retreat from Kabul. He endured nine months of captivity but managed to smuggle his manuscripts and sketches out of Afghanistan, published in 1843 as *Military Operations at Cabul.*

In the 1857 Indian Mutiny, while moving his company of Bengal Artillery from Calcutta up into Oudh, news came through that three native infantry regiments had mutinied and had attacked the civilian population at Arrah (now Ara). He raised the siege and was later involved in the Relief of Lucknow. He died in southern France in 1881.

Captain William de Caux

On Monday, 25 September 1916, the *Eastern Daily Press* received news of the death of Captain William de Caux of the Norfolk Regiment, who was killed in action on 15 September, at the age of 36. He was a well-known figure in Norwich where, until 1909, he was assistant solicitor and managing clerk to Dr E. E. Blyth. The captain's father, who for many years had been a minister of the Catholic Apostolic Church in Paris, frequently resided in Norwich.

William Herring

A Norwich merchant involved in manufacturing, Herring was Sheriff and an Alderman until he became mayor in 1796. He had received a gift of a Spanish sword from Nelson. A member of the Society of United Friars, the Philanthropic Society, and a governor of the Bethel Hospital, he also served as a Poor Law Guardian and a director of the Norwich Union Fire Insurance Society. He had property in Upper King Street and St Giles Street.

Herring served as a captain in the Norfolk Yeomanry and Volunteer Company.

Major David Jamieson, VC, CVO

Jamieson was born in Westminster in 1920, and educated at Eton. In May 1939 he joined the 5th Battalion, Royal Norfolk Regiment (TA). As a 23-year-old captain in the 7th Battalion, Royal Norfolk Regiment, on 7/8 August 1944, in Normandy, Jamieson

was in command of D Company, being the only officer remaining from the company which had established a bridgehead over the River Orne. His company resisted the concentrated counter-attacks of massed Wermacht and SS armour but refused to buckle. His citation reads in part:

> Throughout the thirty-six hours of bitter and close fighting and in spite of the pain of his wounds, Captain Jamieson showed superb qualities of leadership and great personal bravery. There were times when the position appeared hopeless, but on each occasion it was restored by his coolness and determination. He personally was largely responsible for the holding of this important bridgehead over the River Orne and for the repulse of seven German counter-attacks with great loss to the enemy.

Captain David Jamieson.

Captain John Randle VC (Posthumous)

Born in India in 1917, educated at Dragon School, Marlborough College, and Merton College, Oxford (where his best friend was Leonard Cheshire), Randle was commissioned as a subaltern in the Royal Norfolk Regiment in May 1940. While serving with B Company, 2nd Battalion, Royal Norfolk Regiment, he was ordered to assault the Japanese flank at Kohima. His citation reads:

Captain John Randle.

On the 4th May, 1944, at Kohima in Assam, a Battalion of the Royal Norfolk Regiment attacked the Japanese positions on a nearby ridge. Captain Randle took over command of the Company which was leading the attack when the Company Commander was severely wounded. His handling of a difficult situation in the face of heavy fire was masterly and although wounded himself in the knee by grenade splinters he continued to inspire his men by his initiative, courage and outstanding leadership until the Company had captured its objective and consolidated its position. He then went forward and brought in all the wounded men who were lying outside the perimeter. In spite of his painful wound Captain Randle refused to be evacuated and insisted on carrying out a personal reconnaissance with great daring in bright moonlight prior to a further attack by his Company on the position to which the enemy had withdrawn. At dawn on 6th May the attack opened, led by Captain Randle, and one of the platoons succeeded in reaching the crest of the hill held by the Japanese. Another platoon, however, ran into heavy medium machine gun fire from a bunker on the reverse slope of the feature.

Captain Randle immediately appreciated that this particular bunker covered not only the rear of his new position but also the line of communication of the battalion and therefore the destruction of the enemy post was imperative if the operation was to succeed. With utter disregard of the obvious danger to himself Captain Randle charged the Japanese machine gun post single-handed with rifle and bayonet. Although bleeding in the face and mortally wounded by numerous bursts of machine gun fire he reached the bunker and silenced the gun with a grenade thrown through the bunker slit. He then flung his body across the slit so that the aperture should be completely sealed. The bravery shown by this officer could not have been surpassed and by his self-sacrifice he saved the lives of many of his men and enabled not only his own Company but the whole Battalion to gain its objective and win a decisive victory over the enemy.

WOII George Gristock VC (Posthumous)

Warrant Officer 2nd Class Gristock was born in Pretoria, South Africa in 1905 and was serving as CSM in the 2nd Battalion, Royal Norfolk Regiment (BEF) during the fall of France and the Low Countries in May 1940. His citation reads:

> For most conspicuous gallantry on the 21st May 1940, when his company was holding a position on the line of the River Escaut, south of Tournai. After a prolonged attack, the enemy succeeded in breaking through beyond the company's right flank which was consequently threatened. Company Sergeant-Major Gristock having organised a party of eight riflemen from company head-quarters, went forward to cover the right flank.
>
> Realising that an enemy machine-gun had moved forward to a position from which it was inflicting heavy casualties on his company, Company Sergeant-Major Gristock went on, with one man as connecting file, to try to put it out of action. Whilst advancing, he came under heavy machine-gun fire from the opposite bank and was severely wounded in both legs, his right knee being badly smashed. He nevertheless gained his fire position, some twenty yards from the enemy machine-gun post, undetected, and by well-aimed rapid fire killed the machine-gun crew of four and put their gun out of action. He then dragged himself back to the right flank position from which he refused to be evacuated until contact with the battalion on the right had been established and the line once more made good.
>
> By his gallant action, the position of the company was secured, and many casualties prevented. Company Sergeant-Major Gristock has since died of his wounds.

Corporal Sidney Bates VC (Posthumous)

Sidney Bates was born in Camberwell, London in 1921 to Frederick, a rag and bone man, and Gladys May Bates. Bates was working as a carpenter's labourer before joining the army. In 1940 he was serving with the 1st Battalion, Royal Norfolk Regiment. His citation reads:

Corporal Sidney Bates.

In North-West West Europe on 6th August, 1944, the position held by a battalion of the Royal Norfolk Regiment near Sourdeval was attacked in strength by 10th S.S. Panzer Division. The attack started with a heavy and accurate artillery and mortar programme on the position which the enemy had, by this time, pin-pointed. Half an hour later the main attack developed and heavy machine-gun and mortar fire was concentrated on the point of junction of the two forward companies. Corporal Bates was commanding the right forward section of the left forward company which suffered some casualties, so he decided to move the remnants of his section to an alternative position whence he appreciated he could better counter the enemy thrust. However, the enemy wedge grew still deeper, until there were about 50 to 60 Germans, supported by machine guns and mortars, in the area occupied by the section. Seeing that the situation was becoming desperate, Corporal Bates then seized a light machine-gun and charged the enemy, moving forward through a hail of bullets and splinters and firing the gun from his hip. He was almost immediately wounded by machine-gun fire and fell to the ground, but recovered himself quickly, got up and continued advancing towards the enemy, spraying bullets from his gun as he went. His action by now was having an effect on the enemy riflemen and machine gunners but mortar bombs continued to fall all around him.

He was then hit for the second time and much more seriously and painfully wounded. However, undaunted, he staggered once more to his feet and continued towards the enemy who were now seemingly nonplussed by their inability to check him. His constant firing continued until the enemy started to withdraw before him. At this moment, he was hit for the third time by mortar bomb splinters, a wound that was to prove mortal. He again fell to the ground but continued to fire his weapon until his strength failed him. This was not, however, until the enemy had withdrawn and the situation in this locality had been restored.

Corporal Bates died shortly afterwards of the wounds he had received, but, by his supreme gallantry and self sacrifice he had personally restored what had been a critical situation

Lieutenant George Knowland VC (Posthumous)

Knowland was born in 1922 in Catford, Kent. He joined the Royal Norfolk Regiment in 1940 as a private and was commissioned in 1941. He was attached to No. 1 Commando in Burma and earned his VC during the Battle of Hill 170. *The London Gazette* quotes:

On 31 January 1945 near Kangaw, Burma, Lieutenant Knowland was in command of a forward platoon of a troop which was being heavily attacked – some 300 of the enemy concentrating on his 24 men. During the attacks he moved among the men distributing ammunition and contributing with rifle fire and throwing grenades at the enemy. When the crew of one of his forward Bren light machine guns had been wounded, he rushed forward to man it himself. The enemy was only 10 yards away but below the level of the trench so to fire into them he stood up. He continued to fire until the casualties had been evacuated. A replacement gun team that had been sent for were injured while moving up and he stayed with the gun until a third team arrived.

In a subsequent attack he took over a 2 inch mortar which he fired from the hip directly into the enemy. He returned to the trench for more ammunition and fired the mortar from out in the open. When this was used up he fired his rifle. The enemy were then very close and without time to reload his rifle, he picked up a 'Tommy gun' and used it. He killed more of the enemy but received mortal wounds. Despite over 50 per cent losses in the platoon the remainder held on. By the time they were relieved the men had held the ground for 12 hours; they prevented the enemy from advancing further on that hill.

Lieutenant George Knowland.   His grave is in the Taukkyan War Cemetery, Burma.

5. REGIMENTS AND SQUADRONS

Artillery Volunteers, 1859–1908

The 1st Norfolk Artillery Volunteer Corps (AVC) was formed on 29 September 1859 at Great Yarmouth. In November, the 1st Administrative Brigade of Norfolk Artillery Volunteers was formed, which included the 2nd Norfolk AVC, in which two batteries were formed of the Norwich men of the 1st Norfolk AVC, 1869. The volunteers were reorganized in 1880, as 3rd and 4th batteries, Norwich Norfolk (former 2nd) Corps.

Anti-Aircraft Regiment

In 1938, many field artillery units were selected for conversion to an anti-aircraft (AA) role and the Norwich unit was retitled the 78th (1st East Anglian) Anti-Aircraft Regiment, RA. The new regiment was headquartered at All Saints' Green, and comprised 243rd (2nd Norfolk) AA Battery and 244th (3rd Norfolk) AA Battery.

Royal Norfolk Regiment

Formed in 1685 by Henry Cornwall, and known as Henry Cornwall's Regiment of Foot, the regiment participated in the Monmouth Rebellion campaign, when King Charles II's illegitimate son, James Scott, the 1st Duke of Monmouth, tried, but failed to overthrow James II. The regiment was only known as the Royal Norfolk Regiment for twenty-four years. By 1881, under the Childers Reforms of the British army, all the numbered infantry regiments were given geographical links, so the regiment became the Norfolk Regiment. Their headquarters, Britannia Barracks, was built in Norwich. In 1935, and on his Silver Jubilee, George V, Colonel-in-Chief of the regiment, conferred the title 'Royal' on the regiment. In 1959, the 1st East Anglian Regiment was formed from an amalgamation with the Suffolk Regiment, becoming the 1st (Norfolk, Suffolk and Cambridgeshire) Battalion.

It is thought that Queen Anne awarded the figure Britannia to the regiment for gallantry displayed during the Battle of Almanza in 1707, although no evidence of this is available today. However, this letter was received by the colonel of the 9th Regiment of Foot in 1799:

Horse Guard

30th July 1799

Sir, I have received His Royal Highness the Commander in Chief's directions
to signify to you that His Majesty has been pleased to confirm to the ninth
Regiment of Foot the distinction and privilege of bearing the figure 'Britannia'
as the badge of the Regiment.

I have, etc.

(Signed) H. Calvert

Adjutant General

The regiment took the motto 'Firm' after the Battle of Almanza, while
25 April, which was the day of the battle, became the regimental day. 'Holy
Boys' was a nickname that was given to the regiment when Spanish troops
thought that the figure of Britannia on the soldiers' badges was the Virgin
Mary. When William of Orange was invited to take the English throne, the
new colonel, Oliver Nicholas, refused to give allegiance and was replaced by
John Cunningham.

Norfolk Yeomanry

This regiment was raised in 1901, at the express wish of the newly crowned
Edward VII. It was given the title The Norfolk (King's Own) Imperial Yeomanry,
with the Royal cypher as its badge. It was later retitled the King's Own Royal
Regiment (Norfolk Yeomanry). Under the Territorial and Reserve Forces Act
1907, which brought the Territorial Force into being, the force was first intended
as a home defence force for service during wartime. However, at the outbreak of
war on 4 August 1914, many members went on to volunteer for imperial service,
so the territorial battalions split in August and September 1914 into a first line,
which was liable for overseas service, and a second line, which became the home
service for those unable or not willing to serve overseas. At a later period, a third
line was formed to act as a reserve, providing trained replacements for the first-
and second-line battalions.

1/1st Norfolk Yeomanry

In September 1915, the battalion arrived on RMS *Olympic* at Gallipoli with
25 officers and 504 men. Units from the Norfolk Yeomanry were among the last
to be evacuated from the Suvla beach on 20 December. The battalion was then

re-equipped and sent to the Suez Canal, before joining the Western Frontier Force in July 1916 to defend Egypt against the Senussi. In May 1918, the unit was sent to France.

2/1st Norfolk Yeomanry

This battalion was formed in 1914. The following year, it became part of the 2/1st Eastern Mounted Brigade in Huntingdon. Numbered as 13th Mounted Brigade, it joined the 4th Mounted Division in the Wivenhoe area. By 1916, the unit had become a cyclist unit in the 5th Cyclist Brigade, 2nd Cyclist Division. In November of that year, it merged with the 2/1st Suffolk Yeomanry and to form the 7th (Suffolk and Norfolk) Yeomanry Cyclist Regiment in the 3rd Cyclist Brigade.

3/1st Norfolk Yeomanry

The battalion was formed in 1915, and affiliated to a reserve cavalry regiment in Eastern Command. A year later, it was attached to the 3rd Line Groups of the East Anglian Division. Disbanded in 1917, its strength was transferred to the second-line battalion of the 4th (Reserve) Battalion of the Norfolk Regiment, based at Halton Park, Tring.

6th Battalion

At the outbreak of the Second World War, the 6th Battalion was known as the City of Norwich Battalion. Under the command of Lieutenant Colonel D. G. Buxton, it was mobilized at the Aylsham Road Drill Hall. As soon as the battalion was mobilized, A and B companies were sent to Hemsby, while C Company took up guard duties at Watton airfield. The remainder of the battalion stayed in Norwich.

RAF Attlebridge

This was first used by No. 2 Group, Bomber Command, RAF, in 1941. Other units, such as No. 88 Squadron, flew Blenheim IVs and Bostons. In 1942, it was given the United States Army Air Force (USAAF) designation, Station 120, which became part of Eighth Air Force's 2nd Bomb Wing, whose role was heavy bombing. American flying units were also present, having arrived on 12 September 1942 from Harding Army Field in Louisiana, such as the 319th Bombardment Group that flew Martin B-26 Marauders. The station later became a satellite field for RAF Horsham St Faith, which was where most of the personnel were based. It then became a training ground, using Consolidated B-24 Liberator aircraft.

Norfolk Yeomanry recruitment poster, First World War.

RAF Coltishall

The station was a V Bomber dispersal airfield. Cropmarks have been found showing a Roman settlement to the south. Such indicators of agricultural activity continued into medieval times and later at what was known as Scottow Moor (which provided the agricultural land for Scottow Hall). In 1938 a large potato field came up for sale, and plans were announced to build an airfield on it. A year later plans for six hangars were produced, although one was destroyed during the construction. It was renamed Coltishall after the local railway station. By 1940, Spitfires and Hawker Hurricanes had arrived, and in July of that year, Douglas Bader, who had already been fitted with artificial legs, took command of No. 242 Squadron. During the Battle of Britain, Coltishall squadrons acted in a supporting role defending coastal convoys. The same year, RAF Neatishead opened an air-defence station to protect against Luftwaffe raids on industrial and military targets in Norwich. By VE Day, 8 May 1945, Coltishall fighters had damaged over 100 enemy aircraft and destroyed 207. Five years later jet aircraft in the form of de Havilland Vampires were stationed at Coltishall.

From 1963, for a period of thirteen years, the Battle of Britain Memorial Flight was based at Coltishall. In 1964, Coltishall became home to a training squadron of English Electric Lightnings having previously been a frontline fighter station. It was a proud moment for RAF Coltishall in 1967 when it was granted the Freedom of the City of Norwich. By 1982, Sea King helicopters were stationed there during the Falklands conflict. Sad news came in 1983 when six airmen from Coltishall were killed in a coach crash in Germany. In 1987 it saw Concorde land.

The Coltishall Jaguars were based there in 1990, and fought in the First Gulf War in Operation Granby. In 2006, after being in service for sixty-six years, the base closed and became Ministry of Defence Coltishall under Defence Estates. The Jaguar gate guardian was moved to County Hall, Norwich, and a year later, the whole site was sold to the Ministry of Justice. It became a prison – HMP Bure – and the site was bought by Norfolk County Council in 2012.

RAF Fersfield

Sixteen miles south-west of Norwich, Fersfield is most notable as the operational airfield for Operation Aphrodite, a secret plan for using stripped-down, war-weary bombers as explosive-packed, radio-controlled flying bombs, codenamed BQ-7 and BQ-8. Pilots would take off manually and then parachute to safety, leaving the bomber under radio control from another aircraft. One such mission resulted in a plane exploding over the village of Blythburgh in Suffolk, killing Lieutenant Joseph P. Kennedy Jnr, brother of future US president John F. Kennedy. In January 1945, the Aphrodite project was abandoned as being unfeasible. Today, the land has returned to agricultural use. The perimeter track and runways still exist, and a number of wartime buildings remain on the former airfield and in the wooded areas to the south.

RAF Hardwick

Hardwick airfield lies just south of Topcroft village, five miles east of the A140 and twelve miles south of Norwich. Originally built for the RAF, it was first used by the USAAF as designated Station 104. It was home to the 310th Bombardment Group (Medium) from September to November 1942. They were followed by the 93rd Bombardment Group (Heavy) – known as Ted's Travelling Circus – who made it their base for the rest of the war until June 1945. A memorial stands in a small plot on one of the old barracks' sites just off the lane from Hempnall, which runs to the east of the airfield.

RAF Hethel

Now home to Lotus Cars, the former airfield at Hethel is situated on the A11, seven miles south-west of Norwich. The 320th Bombardment Group (Medium) arrived in September 1942, followed in the spring of 1943 by elements of 310th Bombardment Group (Medium). In June that year, the 389th Bombardment Group (Heavy) – nicknamed the Sky Scorpions – arrived.

RAF Horsham St Faith

Just on the outskirts of Norwich, this site operated from 1939 to 1963 as a Royal Air Force station. It was first used by the Blenheim bombers of a detachment of No. 21 Squadron, who had been based at RAF Watton for the last two months of 1939. The Spitfire fighters of No. 19 Squadron, whose flying officer was Douglas Bader, arrived at the start of 1940, and were soon joined by No. 66 Squadron. By the end of May, both squadrons left, with No. 19 going to RAF Duxford and No. 66 to RAF Coltishall. In August, No. 114 moved on to RAF Oulton, a satellite station to Horsham.

RAF Marham

As a Second World War station, it was a base for the de Havilland Mosquito, Vickers Wellington I and the Handley Page Hampden.

6. BARRACKS AND BUILDINGS

Augustine Steward House

On the far side of Tombland, is this picturesque medieval building, a wonderful example of a Tudor merchant's house. It was built – or perhaps, rebuilt – around 1530 by a wealthy mercer named Augustine Steward, who would go on to serve three times as mayor of Norwich. Most famously, the house was used as the headquarters of royal troops sent to quash Robert Kett's Rebellion in 1549. The house is now used by several antique dealers, and is one of the most-photographed buildings in Norwich.

Aviation Museum

In 1977 select members from the Eastern Counties Omnibus Company were invited to become part of an aviation enthusiasts' organization at a museum that would go on to offer membership to all non-employees. A site was acquired

Augustine Steward House.

at Norwich Airport. Soon many exhibits were on show, including the Vulcan bomber. The museum moved to its present site in 1985, where it received over 20,000 visitors that year, who particularly enjoyed viewing the Lockheed T-33.

Barrack Loke

The start of Dragoon Street was marked by a set of steps. The other end was located near the Ranger's House, very near Gurney Road and the Britannia Road junction. Now hidden by trees, is what was a cavalry way. This has changed over time, but what remains is an important link to the military in Victorian and Edwardian Norwich. Nearby, next to Zaks Restaurant, is the fountain ground where many a soldier had a strip torn off him by the sergeant.

Britannia Barracks

Britannia Barracks was built on Mousehold Heath, using the architectural style of Norma Shaw, as the depot for the Royal Norfolk Regiment between 1885 and 1887. The name of the barracks comes from the badge of the regiment. During and after the Second World War, Britannia Barracks, and a few huts behind Nelson Barracks, were turned into an initial training centre for recruits. After basic training, the

Britannia Barracks. (Photo Michael Button)

Britannia Barracks, 1959.

men were sent to the Royal Norfolk Regiment and moved to Nelson Barracks, now known as Corps Training, where they were housed in cavalry barrack blocks.

After the war, the training staff were drawn from the Royal Norfolk and Dorset regiments. These two regiments have maintained a close association over the years, as the Dorset Regiment – the 39th and 54th regiments of foot – had its beginnings in the West Norfolk Regiment of 1782. The regiment amalgamated with the Suffolk Regiment to form the 1st East Anglian Regiment in 1959, and relocated to barracks in Bury St Edmunds. The barracks today survive as the prison, HMP Norwich.

Cavalry Drill Ground

The Cavalry Drill Ground, which is now occupied by houses of the Heartsease Estate, was the Norwich civil airport between the wars. Dragoon Street gave the troops access to Mousehold Heath whence they would have marched into Barrack Street and then Barrack Loke, which is now St James's Close. Now, a set of steps stands at what was once the start of Dragoon Street.

Cow Tower

One of the earliest military structures in the city is that of Cow Tower, which still stands today. Originally built 1398/9 to house artillery, its garrison defended the approach to the city from across the River Wensum. It was specially built to be over

15 metres tall, so that it could overlook the high ground on the opposite bank. It was also built to accommodate the recently developed cannons, along with the customary arrow loops that were used for small guns and crossbows. Other defensive structures in Norwich existed, but Cow Tower was built as an addition. Its ground floor may have been used as a communal dining area, with sleeping quarters on the upper two levels. Its original name was Cowholme, as cows would use the area for grazing.

Nelson Barracks

All that is left today of Nelson Barracks is a wall at the corner of Gurney Road and Barrack Street. Originally the Cavalry Barracks in 1791, the name was changed to honour Lord Horatio Nelson. The barracks was built with horse stables on the ground floor, while the men had their accommodation above. During times of war the men shared the stables until they graduated to the first floor. There was also an officers' mess, nine bay houses, a riding school and administrative buildings. For a long time, many cavalry regiments were garrisoned in Norwich, including the 7th Dragoon Guards, known as Princess Royal's, which saw Norwich as their spiritual home. Right up to the 1950s, Norwich was a garrison town, with many cavalrymen settling in the city after finishing their time in uniform. There was a great affection between the city of Norwich and the regiment, as can be witnessed by the memorials that may be found in the north transept and north aisle of the nave of the cathedral. Church parades meant that the procession of Lancers or the Dragoon Guards between the barracks and Cathedral Close provided a wonderful sight for all to see on a Sunday.

Norwich Cathedral

During the English Civil War, the cathedral was reputedly used as a stable by Roundhead troops who were notorious for defacing religious buildings, and the walls appear to bear testament to this turbulent time. In many areas of the building, it is still possible to clearly make out long lists of names and initials, all with dates that link them to this period.

St Peter Mancroft

Most buildings in Norwich were ill-prepared for Luftwaffe air raids at the outbreak of the Second World War, including St Peter Mancroft. A few young men from the church had already been conscripted for military service, while many others were serving with the TA or were pledged to the Civil Defence and other forms of service. Mancroft was a church with many stained-glass windows, so it was not considered safe, thus resulting in the congregation shrinking. The Sunday school was also closed. After two weeks into the war, the curate, the Reverend Sam Cook, went to serve as an army chaplain, during which time he was awarded the Military Cross for bravery. Vicar Hugh McMullen, a serving officer from the First World War, was not allowed the chaplaincy as he was disabled and living on a disability pension. The glass windows were removed and deposited in the crypt of a church in Somerset, where they remained until December 1947.

During the heavy raids of April 1942, several of Mancroft's windows were damaged, with the west window on the south side completely demolished. The north porch window was blown in, with much damage to the tower.

The Guildhall

This historic building is on Gaol Hill, and is the largest surviving medieval civic building in the country outside London. It served as the seat of the city's government from the early fifteenth century until 1938, when this role transferred to the then new City Hall. According to historic sources, it was built from 'flint, rubble faced with knapped flint and infill'. The east side was crafted from 'alternate squares of faced flint and ashlar stone', presenting a chequered effect. Robert and William Kett spent their last night here before their execution on 7 December 1549.

Norwich Guildhall.

7. LEST WE FORGET

There are over 700 parishes in Norfolk that have a First World War memorial. The Royal Norfolk Regimental Museum has put together a community project where all the memorials are photographed.

Boer War Memorial

In between the castle and ITV Anglia, stands the tall Boer War Memorial constructed of Portland stone. The square base has low steps on each side. It lists on bronze panels all those who died in battle. Each corner features a Corinthian pillar, with shelves and an entablature. The top features a globe, which houses a bronze angel. This beautiful memorial is by George Wade.

Unveiling of the South African War Memorial, 1904.

Chapel Field Memorial

The first death of a church member from the circuit was reported in March 1915. Private Lambert from Rosebery Road United Methodist Church in Norwich, who had enlisted in the Royal Army Medical Corps (RAMC), died from 'spotted fever' in Ipswich Hospital and was buried in Norwich Cemetery. The service was taken by the superintendent minister from Norwich, the Reverend Alfred Bromley, who said, 'The Military authorities desired to honour our brother with a military funeral, but in deference to the parents' wishes, the matter was not pressed, and beyond the presence of a number of the military, the interment was of a private character.'

In September 1915, Lance Corporal G. Varvel of the 1st Battalion, the Norfolk Regiment, was reported to have been wounded, while Private W. H. Randell of the 3rd Battalion had been gassed. In the April 1916 battalion magazine, sympathy was extended to Mr Arthur Gunton on the death of his eldest son at the front. The following month, the magazine carried news of the death of Lance Corporal Frederick James Long, a former Sunday school scholar and member of the Band of Hope, who had joined the army in the first week of the war. He was blown up by a mine at Arras. Leonard Ames of the Norfolk Regiment was reported to have been killed at the Somme on 1 July, and his brother, Ernest, wounded. After some weeks in hospital, he recovered sufficiently to return to light duties with the 11th Suffolks. Two more old scholars and Band of Hope members, James Payne and Charlie Boyce, were also killed in France in July. Another Sunday school boy, Bertie Smith of the Norfolk Regiment, was killed at Delville Wood during the Somme Offensive. Walter Marshall was also killed in action in 1916 on the Western Front.

Footballers and the First World War

51731 Sgt Thomas Allsopp, The Queen's (Royal West Surrey Regiment), tsfd. to (75012) 126th Coy. Labour Corps, 7 March 1919, buried Norwich Cemetery. Played for Brighton & Hove Albion, Leicester Fosse, Luton Town and Norwich City.

8266 Pte James Chalmers, 1/4th Battalion, Royal Scots Fusiliers, 12 July 1915, Helles Memorial, Gallipoli, Turkey. No known grave. Played for Norwich City, Notts County, Preston North End, Sunderland, Swindon Town, Tottenham Hotspur and Watford.

19009 Pte Ernest Edgar Ellis, 16th Battalion, Royal Scots, 1 July 1916, Thiepval Memorial, France. No known grave. Played for Barnsley, Heart of Midlothian and Norwich City.

23245 Sgt William Fiske, 8th Battalion, Border Regiment, 27 May 1918, Soissons Memorial, France. No known grave. Played for Blackpool, Norwich City and Nottingham Forest.

M/288065 Pte John Flanagan, 816th MT Coy, Royal Army Service Corps, 31 August 1917, Dar es Salaam War Cemetery. Played for Arsenal, Fulham and Norwich City.

The Norwich Memorial during the Great War.

F/2726 L/Cpl George Oscar Porter, 18th Battalion, Duke of Cambridge's Own (Middlesex Regiment) 14 July 1918, Esquelbecq Military Cemetery, France. Played for Luton Town, Millwall and Norwich City.

Capt Vivian Sumner Simpson, 12th Battalion, York and Lancaster Regiment, 13 April 1918, Outtersteene Communal Cemetery Extension, Bailleul, France. Played for Norwich City and The Wednesday.

Horatio Nelson

This statue was originally erected near the Guildhall, opposite the entrance of Dove Street. It shows Nelson in the full dress uniform of a vice-admiral, complete with epaulettes and three stars on the cuff. Standing with his left leg placed forward, his empty right sleeve from the arm that he lost in 1797 is pinned to his uniform. He is seen resting a telescope on a cannon with a rope hawser. Weather and wear and tear have eroded a lot of the original features. It was first exhibited in St Andrew's Hall on 19 February 1852. It was moved from its position on Dove Street on 16 April 1856, to opposite the grammar school in Cathedral Close. It was here that Nelson had been a pupil. The decision to move the statue was at the suggestion of Sir Richard Westmacott, who had passed on to the town council a letter from the Honourable Secretary of the Nelson Statue Committee, dated 24 March 1856.

Duke of Wellington

Situated in the beautiful grounds of Norwich Cathedral, is the Grade II-listed statue of the Duke of Wellington. This life-size sculpture was created in 1854 by C. C. Adams. Field Marshal Arthur Wellesley, 1st Duke of Wellington KG, GCB, GCH, PC, FRS, was born on either 29 April or 1 May 1769, a leading Anglo-Irish military and political figure of the nineteenth century. Since his death, there have been many dukes of Wellington, but Arthur Wellesley will always be affectionately remembered as *the* duke. Joining the British army in 1787, he served in Ireland, twice becoming Lord Lieutenant. He was also an MP in the Irish House of Commons. He was a prominent general during the Napoleonic Wars and promoted to field marshal. After Napoleon's exile in 1814, he became duke, serving after the Battle of Waterloo as ambassador to France. He was elected prime minister in 1828 and again in 1834.

Horatio Nelson Memorial at Norwich Cathedral.

Duke of Wellington Memorial at Norwich Cathedral. (Photo Tanya Dedyukhina)

Norwich War Memorial

The Norwich War Memorial is also known as the Norwich Cenotaph, or Norwich City War Memorial. Unveiled in 1927, its original position was outside the Guildhall. It was moved to its present location in 1938. In 2004, the memorial, neglected and in a state of disrepair, was deemed unstable and was closed for seven years while repairs were undertaken. The memorial was turned to face City Hall, and was rededicated on Armistice Day 2011. It is Grade II listed, as are all Lutyens' war memorials. The design, by architect Sir Edwin Lutyens, was the last of his eight cenotaphs erected in England. Lutyens was the leading English architect of his generation. There were several proposals for a memorial prior to Lutyens. In 1926, Lord Mayor Charles Bignold wanted the memorial built before his term in office was over, so he set up the Joint Hospitals and War Memorial Appeal to raise funds.

Norwich City Hall houses the roll of honour listing the names of 3,544 men from Norwich who died in the First World War. Designed by Lutyens, it is made of oak panels, making it unique as there are no other rolls of honour anywhere in the country to match it. It was originally housed in the Norwich Castle keep in 1931.

'Our Glorious Dead': Norwich War Memorial.

'Our Glorious Dead': Norwich War Memorial.

Edith Cavell

Edith Louisa Cavell, born on 4 December 1865, was a nurse who saved the lives of soldiers on both sides during the First World War and helped Allied soldiers escape German-occupied Belgium. Arrested, court-martialled, found guilty of treason and sentenced to death, she was executed on 12 October 1915 by German firing squad in Brussels.

In 1907 Dr Antoine Depage recruited Edith as matron of the nursing school L'École Belge d'Infirmières Diplômées situated on the Rue de la Culture, Ixelles, in Brussels. By 1910 Edith was producing the journal *L'infirmière*. Back in Norfolk at the family home when the First World War broke out, she returned to Belgium and began aiding British soldiers escape to neutral Holland. Through Edith, some 200 Allied soldiers and a hundred Belgian and French civilians of military age were placed in secret houses and provided with false papers by Prince Reginald de Croy at Bellignies near Mons.

Edith Cavell.

Arrested on 3 August 1915 and charged with harbouring Allied soldiers, Edith was held at Saint-Gilles prison for ten weeks. She realized that she had been betrayed by Gaston Quien, who would later be convicted by a court in France as a collaborator. Edith admitted her charges. The government in Britain was not able to help and Sir Horace Rowland of the Foreign Office said, 'I am afraid that it is likely to go hard with Miss Cavell; I am afraid we are powerless.' The under-secretary for foreign affairs, Lord Robert Cecil, stated, 'Any representation by us will do her more harm than good.' The German civil governor, Baron von der Lancken, stated that Edith should be pardoned because she had also helped so many German soldiers and had been so honest, but to no avail.

On the evening of her execution Edith received Holy Communion from Reverend Stirling Gahan. She said, 'Patriotism is not enough. I must have no hatred or bitterness towards anyone.' The final words were given to the German Lutheran prison chaplain Paul le Seur: 'Ask Father Gahan to tell my loved ones later on that my soul, as I believe, is safe, and that I am glad to die for my country.'

When the war was over her body was taken back to England. She was given a state funeral at Westminster Abbey before her body was transferred to Norwich Cathedral. A graveside service is still held each year on 12 **October** as well as an annual flower festival in her village of Swardeston. The work that Edith started is still in existence today, under the Cavell Nurses' Trust.

Shot at dawn

John Henry Abigail was born to Susannah Maria and John James Abigail on 29 April 1897 in Thorpe Hamlet, Norwich. Before the start of the Great War, the family moved to Distillery Yard just off Oak Street. The National Society for the Prevention of Cruelty to Children had been keeping an eye on the family and when a visit was made the children were seen to be of ill health and in a poor state from vermin bites. Mr and Mrs Abigail were taken to court where Mrs Abigail was found not guilty, but Mr Abigail was sent to Norwich Prison for one month.

John Henry was conscripted in March 1916 and fought with the 8th Battalion, Norfolk Regiment at Delville Wood where, on 19 July 1916, the battalion suffered eighty dead, thirty missing and 180 wounded, one of which was

John Henry Abigail.

John Henry. Repatriated to England to recuperate, he went AWOL for eight days in in December 1916 to assist his three siblings in the workhouse, both his alcoholic parents now in prison. Arrested on Boxing Day, he was sentenced to 168 hours' detention and forfeiture of nine days' pay.

In January 2017, he again went AWOL to assist in a family crisis. He voluntarily surrendered himself at Britannia Barracks. In addition to detention and loss of pay, he was sentenced to fourteen days' Field Punishment No. 1: manacled to the wheel of a gun carriage dressed only in shirt and breeches for several hours a day, this in the harshest winter in living memory.

Back on the Western Front by April 1917, he deserted just prior to the battle of Arras. He was captured eight days later and at the court martial received ten years' penal servitude pending review. During the Third Ypres offensive, on 30 July 1917, as the 8th Norfolks were waiting to 'go over the top' at Passchendaele, John Henry again deserted. Soon arrested in the French village of Staple, his court martial took place on the 24 August; during the case he did not speak or ask anyone to speak for him.

Private 9694 Abigail J. H. was sentenced to death and shot at dawn on Wednesday 12 September 1917 by his B Company comrades who had drawn lots for inclusion in the firing squad. He was twenty years old. In November 2006, along with 306 executed servicemen from the Great War, Private Abigail received an official pardon from the British government.

St Peter Mancroft

The FEOPOW stands for the Norwich Fellowship of ex-POWs, an organization that remembers the fall of Singapore in the Second World War. Thousands of East Anglian servicemen became Japanese POWs.

The service held on Sunday, 4 November 1945 was the first special thanksgiving for the returned ex-FEPOWs and their families. During the service, Percy Mark Herbert, Bishop of Norwich, gave an address in which he posed the question, 'For what have you been spared?' For many years, that question has been answered by the formation of the National Federation of Far East Prisoners of War Clubs and Associations (NFCCA).

Since 1945, services of thanksgiving and rededication have been held at regular intervals at the church. The pulpit has been used by many clergymen, including Bishop Wilson, who was at one time Bishop of Singapore and who

NFFWRA standard.

was tortured by the Kempeitai. The gathering was to discuss what had been learned as prisoners of the Japanese.

The memorial was designed by David Holgate and cost £1,800. It is an elongated, raised oval in a blue-black Welsh slate, with the insignia of FEPOW freestanding above, with the wording: 'In Memory of the many Comrades who did not return or whose lives were shortened by the conditions of their captivity and

Veterans celebrate the 68th anniversary of VJ Day, Norwich, 2013.

in commemoration of the services of prayer and thanksgiving held here for the Norwich Fellowship of Ex-Far East Prisoners'.

The 68th anniversary of VJ Day took place in St Peter Mancroft Church in Norwich in 2013. Present were the Right Reverend Alan Winton, Bishop of Thetford, who also preached at the service, and Captain Tom Tulloch, Naval Adviser to the Canadian High Commission, Sheriff of Norwich, Mr Graham Creelman, Mrs Vivica Parsons and the FEPOW chaplain, Mrs Pauline Simpson. The Deputy Lord Lieutenant, Mr Charlie Barratt, was also present. Two hundred people attended, including NFFWRA patron Patrick Toosey, the son of Lieutenant Colonel Philip Toosey, who was put in charge of constructing the bridge on the River Kwai by the Japanese.

SOURCES & ACKNOWLEDGEMENTS

The author acknowledges with thanks Archant, Battle of Britain Historical Society, Commonwealth War Graves Commission, Gemma Wassell, Guy's Hospital medical schools' records, HEART, Methodist History, Ian McMullen, Football and the First World War, London Archives, Norfolk's American Connection, Norwich Cathedral, Royal Air Force, Royal Navy Association, St Peter Mancroft Church *Mancroft Review*, and The Royal Anglian Regiment. In addition, the following titles proved particularly useful:

Mottram, R. H., *Assault upon Norwich*. (The Soman-Wherry Press Ltd)

Sutherland, Jon & Canwell, Diane, *The Holy Boys*. (Pen & Sword Military, 2010)

Bates, Martin, *The Regional Military Histories East Anglia*. (Osprey Publishing Ltd, 1974)

Meeres, Frank, *Norfolk in the First World War*. (Phillimore, 2004)

Banger, Joan, *Norwich at War*. (Poppyland Publishing, 2003)

Douglas Brown, R., *East Anglia 1940*. (Terrence Dalton Ltd, 1981)

The Norwich Breweries Second World War Memorial: the names Kett and Armiger are already familiar.

ABOUT THE AUTHOR

Michael Chandler is an author, historian and broadcaster. He was born in Forest Gate, London, in May 1962, and has spent most of his adult working life in the media industry. He moved to Norwich in April 2006 and very quickly fell in love with the area. He has written over a dozen books on Norwich and Norfolk since 2010, his most recent being *Historical Women of Norfolk* (2016). *Great British Military Hospitals of the First World War* is a new book that he is working on for Pen & Sword. He was Historical Adviser to Future Radio and has been involved with Mustard TV, BBC Look East, BBC Radio Norfolk, Radio Norwich and ITV Anglia. As well as writing for several other magazines, Michael is a features writer for *A Fine City* where he is also the restaurant and food critic. A vegetarian and animal lover, Michael's hobbies include history, art, cinema, theatre, reading, cooking, walking and music from the 1960s.